Praise for Fri

"Don't be deceived by what may appear to be delightful, soft spoken 'playlets' which could easily be developed into full length plays. The Fricatives anthology. dives deep and extends wide into complex dilemmas of race, class, gender, and spirituality. Cesi Davidson crafts this inquiry with characters ranging from inanimate objects, to food, to animals. When her characters are human, their authentic dialogue is flavored with magical realism that entrances the reader and spirits them to the end of the tale. Actors are challenged to live the truth of a Green Pea. Directors must create an ensemble which can ferret in and out of time, transporting the audience beyond their wildest imaginings. Designers are invited to build worlds both minimalist, or whimsical, and every way in between. Don't be afraid to surrender your soul, naked to the depth in these plays. Whether read or performed, it's an unforgettable trip."

—Tonya Pinkins, Tony Award Winning Actor and Award winning filmmaker of *RED PILL*

"Cesi Davidson's creativity knows no bounds. Wildly imaginative in style, hilarious, moving, and often disturbing, her plays illuminate a wide range of real-life experiences—human, vegetable, and beyond. Whether seen in production "or read in the privacy of your home, Davidson's plays will introduce you to voices you've never heard, make you think about the world in ways you've never considered, and stir up emotions you never knew you had. What more can you ask of this wonderful writer?"

—Zachary Sklar, Oscar-nominated screenwriter for *JFK* (with Oliver Stone)

"Cesi Davidson's words are musical notes on paper. She creates stories with a composer's tools: rhythm, melody, harmony, timbre, dynamics, texture, and form. Some plays in her anthology Fricatives, have the emotional feel of a familiar ballad. Others are complex symphonies. Still others jump off the page with the energy of boogie woogie. Cesi has found a way to be guided in her writing by the universality of music and language, and the marriage is beautiful."

—John 'JT' Thomas, musician and composer

"The words come through me," says a character in one of Cesi Davidson's marvelous new plays. "I don't own them… or do I?" This character is channeling the spirit of artist Jean-Michel Basquiat, and, in turn, being channeled by the author. Such moments abound here, moments of wonder and wondering. The human voice—that most rich and varied of instruments—breaks through again and again, riffing on our shared reservoir of bliss and heartache and hilarity. These little plays are big."

—John Gould, author of *The End of Me*

"Cesi Davidson's compelling plays in the anthology *Fricatives* are grounded in forgiveness and resilience, permitting emancipation and the freedom to be one's true authentic self. As always, Davidson's work asks us to examine and transform the "nonhuman" aspects of our humanity, liberating ourselves from the poison in our hearts and allowing us to see the full extent of human joy, excellence, and magic."

—Tobie S. Stein, author, of *Racial and Ethnic Diversity in the Performing Arts Workforce*

"Cesi Davidson's short plays will intrigue, delight, move, and shock you. You might be drawn to her whimsical creatures residing in the animal kingdom or the country of fruits and vegetables. You might be drawn to her human characters, the real-world issues of lack of opportunities, discrimination and racism. Whatever your preference, you will be entertained, you will learn from these plays and you will think about them long after you have finished reading/watching them."

—Anna Steegmann, bilingual writer and translator

"The plays in Cesi Davidson's anthology Fricatives are small bites that satisfy a five course gourmet literary palate."

—Celeste Rita Baker, author of *Glass Bottle Dancer*, *De MotherJumpers*, and the short story collection *Back, Belly and Side*

"In this kaleidoscope of plays, you'll meet many characters, human and non-human, that collectively shine a light on humanity with honesty, heartache, and humor. Cesi's imaginative, playful and courageous words are golden for a performer. I especially appreciate the diverse casting that offers fresh perspectives on our shared human experience. These unique voices remind us that the world is full of wonder, and I'll never look at pasta the same way ever again."

—Rachel Lu, actress, *Chingish* and *Front Cover*

"From a pair of frozen peas who take themselves too seriously to an activist cow to an old friend of Jean Michel Basquiat, Cesi Davidson spotlights people and things that may never have otherwise seen the light. You can think you understand a character's motivation, but in an instant they will transform and astound you, leaving you breathless. In this latest collection of Cesi's plays, a reader will find in every piece the "audible friction" that is the title of the book. Many of the darker plays have an incredible lightness, and her lighter pieces offer deeper glimpses into subjects like grief, abuse and greed. She can broach these topics with ease because she knows how to encase them in love. Her cows are righteous, her peas are hard-working, and her words point us towards a more truthful version of ourselves."

—Kim Chinh, actor, screenwriter, playwright, author of *Reclaiming Vietnam*

Fricatives

Conversation Pieces

A Small Paperback Series from Aqueduct Press
Subscriptions available: www.aqueductpress.com

About the Aqueduct Press
Conversation Pieces Series

The feminist engaged with sf is passionately inter-
ested in challenging the way things are, passionately
determined to understand how everything works. It is
my constant sense of our feminist-sf present as a grand
conversation that enables me to trace its existence into
the past and from there see its trajectory extending into
our future. A genealogy for feminist sf would not con-
stitute a chart depicting direct lineages but would offer
us an ever-shifting, fluid mosaic, the individual tiles of
which we will probably only ever partially access. What
could be more in the spirit of feminist sf than to con-
ceptualize a genealogy that explicitly manifests our own
communities across not only space but also time?

Aqueduct's small paperback series, Conversation Pieces,
aims to both document and facilitate the "grand conversation." The Conversation Pieces series presents a wide variety of texts, including short fiction (which may not always
be sf and may not necessarily even be feminist), essays,
speeches, manifestoes, poetry, interviews, correspondence,
and group discussions. Many of the texts are reprinted material, but some are new. The grand conversation reaches at
least as far back as Mary Shelley and extends, in our specu-
lations and visions, into the continually created future. In
Jonathan Goldberg's words, "To look forward to the history that will be, one must look at and retell the history
that has been told." And that is what Conversation Pieces
is all about.

L. Timmel Duchamp

Jonathan Goldberg, "The History That Will Be" in Louise
Fradenburg and Carla Freccero, eds., *Premodern Sexualities* (New
York and London: Routledge, 1996)

Conversation Pieces
Volume 82

Fricatives

Short Plays to Nourish the Mind & Soul

by
Cesi Davidson

Published by Aqueduct Press
PO Box 95787
Seattle, WA 98145-2787
www.aqueductpress.com

For information on licensing rights for production of a
play in this collection contact the author directly:
cesidavidson@gmail.com

ISBN: 978-1-61976-214-5

Cover and all illustrations courtesy Michal Ammar
Cover background, © Can Stock Photo / realcg;

Original Block Print of Mary Shelley by Justin Kempton:
www.writersmugs.com

Printed in the USA by Applied Digital Imaging

For my grandmothers,
Mattie Bushnell and Inez Davidson
Thank you for loving me.

*Fricatives force change
through a narrow channel*

Contents

Foreword

Daniel Judah Sklar
Daniel is the author of PLAYMAKING: Children Writing and Performing Their Own Plays. *Currently he leads classes for the Harlem Dramatic Writing Workshop and is a teaching artist for the Kennedy Center in Washington, DC.*

In the penultimate play of this moving and amusing collection, a character named Cesi calls John Prine, the revered idiosyncratic singer/song writer, in heaven and explains that a person can have 20/20 vision in his or her eyes and still be blind. In order to truly see, one needs a moral heart, she explains. If our hearts are stuffed with hurt and selfishness, the eyes can't do their job properly; the lack of moral vision distorts and thereby blocks reality.

Fortunately for readers of these short dramas and comedies, Cesi Davidson has a pure moral heart. She sees us as we are. And she has the talent to imagine characters who reveal that vision in unexpected and illuminating situations. In some instances they are realistic, like the couple who have been enraged at one another since the death of their son but finally confess their hidden agendas and can go on. In others they are surreal, like a talking cow who is saved from corporate greed by West Indian Frozen Yogurt entrepreneurs. They also can break your heart, like the grandma who did everything right as a student but was denied recognition by nakedly abusive racism—only to be misunderstood years later by her own grandchildren. And still others, who are genuinely frightening, like a carnivorous anthropoid who gives birth and kills with equal vigor.

Davidson's earlier book, *Articulations*, had a similar range of surprising and sympathetic characters in situations that remind us of human aspirations and conflicts, but *Fricatives* goes deeper. The couple whose son dies and the grandma whose grandkids fail to see her are portrayed so vividly that I was not just touched but also deeply moved. The talking cow and her bizarre destiny gave me an understanding of the corporate world that volumes of analysis never could. Seeing the anthropoid in action brought home the danger of uncontrolled technology so vividly that I was shocked.

Conflict is the key to Davidson's dialogue. Her protagonists want something from their antagonists, and they try to get it. The antagonists resist. Action occurs when there is change; one side gets what he/she/it wants or there is a compromise. In these plays the conflicts and subsequent actions also build to climaxes where the characters understand one another and we, the audience, realize what that means.

I believe these plays are joyful and enlightening reading and are the basis for scintillating evenings in the theatre.

Introduction

My father, Charles Davidson was a gifted musician. As a young man, he was offered a scholarship to a prestigious music school. Obligations to the family business prevented his attendance. His family and music were his joy. While working at the C&D Cement Block Company, he continued mastery of all the stringed instruments. The bass violin was his preferred bliss. I remember hearing his tunes from the living room fill our home. He could play it all, from abstract jazz stanzas to Broadway show tunes.

As I watched my siblings become musicians, I wondered why I wasn't blessed with the "music gene." Later in my adult life, I found musical expression through written language: phonetic tones, word stress, and sentence intonation. The dialogue between characters in my plays often mimicked improvisational conversation. I found myself in the company of musicians more. I eventually partnered with one.

In this second anthology of plays, I've assembled an eclectic mix of characters. Each one moves through a life's journey with a rhythm, and a purpose. Each one wants something while exuding a personal style, and a swag. As you read each play, I encourage you to find each character's perspective. Don't walk in their shoes. Move in their stride. Enjoy the strolls.

Cesi Davidson
July 2021

Pasta Mob

To Be Continued

Characters

Detective Escarola Bean Manicotti: Female officer of the law

Checky Ravioli: Sexy female thug/mobster, Cheeky's cousin

Cheeky Ravioli: Sexy female thug/mobster, Checky's cousin

Setting

New York City

Circa today, tomorrow, yesterday

Lights Rise

(The curtains on the stage are drawn closed. Downstage, Detective Escarola Bean Manicotti stands under a streetlight. She wears a trench coat and hat. Her pockets are filled with garlic knots and bread sticks. In front of the curtain, there are two chairs. Checky and Cheeky Ravioli sit on the chairs holding bouquets of flowers. An enormous white bridal veil covers their faces and torsos.)

ESCAROLA: My name is Detective Escarola Manicotti. This is my city. I work for the NYPDHDLMNOP, New York City's finest. And this is my story. (Reaching into pocket) Can I offer you a bread stick? (Walking as she munches, looking into the audience) You… What do you mean, "What's my middle name? What's it to you? You got a middle name? (Pause) Farina Wheatina? Oh…that's ordinarily so pathetic. (Sniffs a garlic knot) The garlic…gets the edge off. A woman in my position is under an extraordinarily sex and stress. Sex, that's another story. (Pause) Look you's…I'll tell you my middle name only for your dictionary encyclopedia like reference purposes. You're never to repeat my middle name. And I won't appreciate you breaking, smashing, and mesmerizing my wishes. You understand what I'm saying? (Taking a deep breath then speaking quietly) Bean. (Pause) What do you mean you didn't hear me? (Speaking quietly) Bean. (Pause) Alright. Alright.

Bean. My full, officiated, personal name—given to me by my mother originated from Queens, and my father originated from Brooklyn born and raised God bless—is Escarola Bean. You got it. Detective Escarola Bean Manicotti. Now forget about it. (Pause) One more thing. So, when I was of a certain age, when I was identifying and discovering my inner spiritual like self, I ask my mother, "Ma, Why should you have to names me Bean? You ruined my whole life." And she says, "I could have been specificated with the bean and named you chick pea. Then you should be greater upset with me and your father because guys would be of the opinion to call you "Chick" for short. You think you got problems now? What if you was to be called, "Chick" for your entire feminine life?" (Pointing to Checky and Cheeky) Oh, them? They's an intimate and very important like part of my intricate story. Say hello, bimbos.

CHECKY & CHEEKY: Hello Bimbos.

ESCAROLA: Hey. Hey. There's some fellas and some whatevers out there.

CHECKY & CHEEKY: Whatevers.

ESCAROLA: Checky and Cheeky Ravioli, cousins ten times removed. Inseparable since they shared a crib as young babes. And now, the most feared thugs in New York City, known professionally collectively as the "Pasta Mob." (Inhaling the garlic from garlic knots) Don't you judge me. I'm not snorting oregano or stuffing my nose with panna cotta.

CHEEKY: Get to the point Escarola.

CHECKY: Yeah, tell them about the weddings.

ESCAROLA: Pipe down your pastarini. (Speaking to audience) They was both left at the altars for reasons I don't know, on the days of their weddings.

(Checky and Cheeky stand and pull off their veils. They're dressed in trench coats, dark sunglasses, and fashionable hats. They throw their flowers into the audience and pick up their designer handbags.)

ESCAROLA: Don't take those flowers. They're cursed.

(Checky and Cheeky move the chairs. Cheeky places a telephone on a telephone stand center stage. Checky collects boxes of pasta and places them in a wheel barrel. Checky exits.)

ESCAROLA: From that pitiful day of their disrupted nuptials they turned to a life of crime. Now, I'm hot on the trail of the Ravioli cousins, whom I suspect are controlling the flow of pasta in the Big Apple. As supplies of pasta are diminishing, violence is rampant in four of the five boroughs: Manhattan, Brooklyn,

7

Queens, and the Bronx. My first clue…Staten Island. They were hit first.

(Exit Escarola to a stake out. She observes the activities on Staten Island.)

CHEEKY: (Takes off her trench coat, dark glasses, and hat, revealing very sexy lingerie. She holds the handset of the telephone.) Hello Auntie Pasto. It's your niece Cheeky Ravioli. Yeah, Checky is okay.

CHECKY: (Enters with the wheel barrel filled with pasta. She removes her trench coat, dark glasses, and hat, revealing her very sexy lingerie) How ya doing Auntie?

CHEEKY: Checky sends her love and her convalescents to you simultaneously.

CHECKY: Tell her I need to borrow some of her blemish concealer.

CHEEKY: Hey. I'm trying to do business here.

CHEEKY: Looking like a beauty is a very important part of our business.

CHEEKY: I needs for you to do me a favor. And for this favor, I should be in debt to you for my life. And my children and their children and their children and their children should be in debt to you the same. Perhaps that debts you multiple grand nieces and nephews for millions of years. I'm not sure. I lost count.

CHECKY: (Arranging the boxes and hiding them back stage) This is the last of the Staten Island pasta.

CHEEKY: We'll move them to the safe house later. Go take a powder.

CHECKY: (Exiting) Tell Auntie she should call Patty Peppers and Sausages for some muscle.

ESCAROLA: (Waking herself up from a garlic knot high) I would know Checky Ravioli's fragrant parfume anywhere. (Pause) It's nothing. I can't smell any pasta. (Looking at Staten Island) From my vantage point, near Lady Liberty, the Statue of Liberty herself, I sees massive exodus of multigenerational types driving, running, skateboarding, fast walking, which is better for your health by the way, across the Verrazano Bridge. No, now they've stopped. There's something preventing them from getting into Brooklyn. Now, everyone is running the other direction, across the Goethals Bridge into Jersey. (Taking notes)

CHEEKY: Me and Checky. We've taken the pasta from Staten Island, and we've incapacitated the bridge. No worries, no civilians have been hurt. They've all gone to Jersey. What I needs for you to do is assemble a meeting of the New York City Gravy Association at the dock of the Staten Island ferry. Call Patty Peppers and Sausages. I need her and her football team to frisk everyone. Make sure no one is carrying heat… hot plates, fry pans, or hair dryers. I need the heads of the families there. All of them. And when me and Checky is finished with this heist, I'll keep my promise that you should remember I made so long ago when I was a kid and you gave me a Suzie Bake Toy Oven. I'm gonna liberate Uncle Ben and Aunt Jemima. (Hangs up the phone) Powder time is over, Checky. Let's get to the ferry.

(Exit Cheeky and Checky)

ESCAROLA: I see a border wall has been erected at the end of the Verrazano Bridge. No Staten Island immigrants can enter Brooklyn where my father was born and raised God bless. And as I'm watching the wall that's there but never been there before...I'm seeing Staten Island sink into the ocean.

(Cheeky and Checking stand on the Staten Island Ferry with members of the New York City Gravy Association.)

CHEEKY: Me and my cousin Checky...

CHECKY: Yeah. Me and my cousin Cheeky...

CHEEKY & CHECKY: We want to welcome yous to this impromptu but not so impromptu meeting of the New York City Gravy Association. (Applause)

CHECKY: Anybody got concealer?

CHEEKY: Thank you for coming. We see so many familiar faces.

CHECKY: And so many new to the industry.

CHEEKY: But one thing we all have in common is our love for pasta.

CHECKY: Mazella Mozzarella and her mother Minnie Minestroni. We welcome yous.

CHEEKY: Carmela Catch Tori, How ya doin?

CHECKY: Penny Pancetta. Can always depend on you.

CHEEKY: Haven't seen you in a long time Stella Stuffed Peppers.

CHECKY: Terry Tiramisu. Always a sweetheart.

CHEEKY: My dear friends, the Cannoli.

CHECKY: Seppole Zeppole.

CHEEKY: Patsy Panettone.

CHECKY: Struffoli Marfoli Mascarpone

CHEEKY: Nice of you to show up in support us, Bruschetta.

CHECKY: And our Auntie Pasto sent the Pepperoni twins from her family just to make sure everything goes the way it should today.

CHEEKY: Betty Bread Crumb and her family wanted to come, but me and Checky didn't think it was necessary. We rely on yous that is here to tell those that is not here our message.

CHEEKY & CHECKY: We're taking over the Pasta.

CHECKY: As we speak, all that existed of pasta on Staten Island is vanished.

CHECKY: All the home cooks who processed the fine art of making homemade pasta have emigrated to New Jersey and will never return. And that's because in about (looking at watch) seven to thirteen minutes Staten Island will be no more.

CHEEKY: No more. Sunk into the ocean from the five hundred thousand pounds of melting Italian ice and gelato that we placed in Freshkills Park. Causing a tsunami of enormous proportions never before seen in this part of New York State.

ESCAROLA: It was there. Now it's gone. Staten Island, may you rest in peace. (Sniffing garlic knots)

CHEEKY: It saddens me that we found ourselves forced to take these drastic steps. We ain't thugs. We're just business women. But you refused to share your profits from the gravies: vodka, puttanesca, marinara, bolongnese, and alfredo. And you rationed our shipments causing great distress for our Manhattan clients in particular.

CHECKY: Yeah. Butter alone on pasta is not always satisfying.

CHEEKY: Pasta and gravy were meant to be married.

CHECKY: Married. Like me and my Vito.

CHEEKY: (Consoling Checky) This what we gonna do. Out of respect for my father born and raised in Brooklyn God bless, and my mother with her heritage from Queens, you'll get a piece of the action in both boroughs but only with tortellini. You'll pay us for a ration of gravy, which my cousin Checky will decide.

CHECKY: Yeah, tortellini is better with butter anyways. For every half pan of tortellini, you'll get a pound of butter. And you'll get one cup of marinara a month.

ESCAROLA: Only one family has the meatballs to carry off a heist, a siege, and alteration of public property all in less than twenty-four hours. The Ravioli cousins. It seems to me that they're gonna make a move into every borough. They started with the least important first. But what is their master plan? Sanitation strikes, blackouts, hurricanes, and economic recession. Nothing will devastate the Big Apple more than no pasta. From this, I don't think New York City can recover. My next step, follow the ferry. Will it go to Manhattan or Brooklyn?

CHEEKY: This ferry will give you safe passage into Bay Ridge bypassing the border wall. As long as we're in agreement, you have nothing to fear from the Raviolis. (Speaking to Checky) We need to split up Checky. The NYPDHDLMNOP is gonna come after us fast and hard.

CHECKY: They got nothing on us.

CHEEKY: Escarola will trace this ingenious work to the Raviolis. We need to be ready.

CHECKY: I'll fix my face.

CHEEKY: You go to the warehouse at the Bruce in Harlem. I'll go to Queens. I'm gonna convince the plum tomato farmers that they should sell only to us. We'll start a tomato famine. We'll capture the tomato paste market.

CHECKY: How you gonna convince them Cheeky?

CHEEKY: Beef stake and grape tomatoes. I'm bringing illegals from the Bronx. Keep the phone line open. Take an inventory of the goods. And Checky, if Escarola busts into our joint, zip your lips.

CHECKY: Sure. But what if I need to replenish my luscious lipgloss?

CHEEKY: Fix it now so you can be ready.

(Exit Cheeky and Checky)

ESCAROLA: I need to infiltrate the gravy association. That means traveling in disguise. (She takes off her trench coat and hat, revealing sexy lingerie.)

(Lights up on Checky on the telephone.)

CHECKY: Yeah?

CHEEKY: Did you calculate the inventory?

CHECKY: Sure.

CHEEKY: What is it?

CHECKY: Sure. (Reading from a clipboard) We got bows, cavatelli, conchiglie, bow ties, fusilli, mezzani the big ones and the little ones, penne, rigatoni, shells, ziti.

CHEEKY: What about the elbows?

CHECKY: Yeah, we got the elbows. But what we need the elbows for?

CHEEKY: Never you so mind about that.

CHECKY: And Cheeky, why haven't you told me where you hiding the spaghetti.

CHEEKY: Don't worry about it. Nobody, I mean nobody will ever get their hands on the spaghetti. (Hangs up phone)

ESCAROLA: I have a delicate choice to make. I need to capture the thugs on the ferry and make them talk and chew at the same time. I need to capture the Raviolis before they do any more damages. I could follow the ferry to Brooklyn, but I could expect every feminine type mob person to have her trap shut in more ways than one. There's another solution. Many years of garlic snorting have resulted in my very delicate nasal palate. (Sniffing) I smell the signature perfume of Checky Ravioli, "Eau de pasta water toilette." If I follow the scent, I'll find Checky. I'll find Checky. And if I find Cheeky, I'll find the goods or visa versa. If I find Cheeky with Checky, the goods will be with the two of them. I'm a little dizzy. (Walking around tracing the scent) You get my meaning?

(Lights up on Checky trying on different pairs of shoes. Then she stands next to the telephone stand and picks up the phone.)

CHECKY: Yeah?

CHEEKY: Is that you Checky? You sound different like.

CHECKY: Yeah, I think it's me.

CHEEKY: Well, how do I know it's you?

CHECKY: I don't know. How do I know it's you?

CHEEKY: Ask me something only me, myself, and I would know. (Pause) Ask me.

CHECKY: I'm thinking. Oh yeah. On what location on my face is my most beautified beauty mark?

CHEEKY: It's a trick question. Your whole face is a beauty mark. You're so gorgeous. (Pause)

CHECKY: What question should you be asking or should I be asking to self-identify your person?

CHEEKY: Tell me about one of my personal garment sizes that I should never want revealed because it's personal.

CHECKY: Your waistline is triple minus double zero.

CHEEKY: Correct. I love you. I may be a little detained if the tomatoes on the vine in Queens are tangled.

CHECKY: I can handle it. (Hangs up phone) She's so sensitive.

(Enter Escarola)

ESCAROLA: Checky Ravioli, the one person of the two-person pasta mob in the flesh.

(Checky holds up her hands) Your fermented pasta water fragrance never dissipates.

CHECKY: Wait just a minute Escarola.

(Checky puts on lip-gloss and then sits on a chair with her hands behind her back.)

ESCAROLA: Where are the goods Checky?

CHECKY: I'll never tell you rubber heels.

ESCAROLA: Well you're gonna tell me this. What's that shade of lip-gloss?

CHECKY: Heavenly-Hell Red.

ESCAROLA: If you weren't so bad, that shade of lip-gloss would be so good for you. I'll ask you for the last time. Where are the goods?

CHECKY: I'll never tell you Escarola…Bean.

ESCAROLA: Who told you my middle name?

CHECKY: Our Auntie Pasto and your mother went to Queens Boulevard High School together. Only your mother never finished.

ESCAROLA: Now I'm really gonna give it to you.

(Escarola punches Checky from side to side. Checky makes joyful sounds.)

ESCAROLA: What's wrong with you? You on aspirin or something?

CHECKY: Don't stop, Escarola. It helps my accu-punch points. Stimulates the muscles in my check tissue.

ESCAROLA: (Picking up a strainer) I'm not fooling around with you, Checky.

CHECKY: What are you doing with the strainer?

ESCAROLA: I'm going to boil some linguine. I took a box out of the evidence room at headquarters.

CHECKY: Cooking linguine is against the law, and you is the law.

ESCAROLA: Sometimes even the law has to break the pasta law for the greater good.

CHECKY: There's only one reason you would bring linguine…for torture.

ESCAROLA: That's right. I'm gonna cook the pasta in front of you. Throw the pasta water down the drain…and then

CHECKY: No.

ESCAROLA: And then…

CHECKY: Please Escarola…even you can't be that cruel.

ESCAROLA: I'm gonna water board the linguine with cold water. I'm gonna rinse it until there's no starch left. Then I'm gonna sit the noodles in a bucket of ice.

CHECKY: (Screaming) I'll tell you what you want to know.

ESCAROLA: Do you have the spaghetti?

CHECKY: We would never touch the spaghetti. It's sacred. It has angel hair. Cheeky shipped it overseas to the Vatican.

ESCAROLA: Then where's the other pasta? Tell me. Give up the goods Checky.

CHECKY: Promise me. Promise me. You won't rinse the linguine.

ESCAROLA: Give up the goods.

CHECKY: It's in the Bruce vault.

ESCAROLA: Unlock the vault.

CHECKY: You'll have to untie me.

ESCAROLA: Checky, you never been tied.

(Checky gets up from the chair and goes behind the stage curtain. She draws the drapes, revealing hundreds of boxes of pasta.)

CHECKY: It's all here. Every box, from every borough except the Bronx. We was doing that last because of some negotiations we was making with the rice and beans. (Sitting down weeping) You're cruel Escarola. Pasta should never be rinsed. Without starch, pasta can never marry gravy. Just like Vito Scarapini Scarpari-ello Scarparo and me.

17

ESCAROLA: Who did you say?

CHECKY: Vito Scarapini Scarpariello Scarparo Parmesan was my one true love. And on the day of our planned nuptials he didn't show up at City Hall. I don't understand it. He loved me. I loved him.

ESCAROLA: Vito Scarapini Scarpariello Scarparo Parmesan was my brother.

CHECKY: Your brother?

ESCAROLA: He told me he was gonna secretly marry a girl who was in a lot of trouble. His plan was to move with her to a gated community in Nassau County Long Island. He called her his "Baby Arugula."

CHECKY: That's me. Arugula Arogula Argencha Ravioli. Checky is my business name.

ESCAROLA: That means that you…

CHECKY: That means that you…

ESCAROLA & CHECKY: Sister in laws…in the law…

ESCAROLA: Vito overdosed on olive bread. We found him on Arthur Avenue in the Bronx, before the nuptials.

(Enter Cheeky)

CHEEKY: Not so fast. Both of yous hands up. Then sit down. Then hands on your laps. Cross your legs. Escarola, garlic knot addict detective. And Checky, wanna be mob boss but you ain't got the smarts. I pretended to be in love with Vito so I could destroy you and Bean. We met on Arthur Avenue for meals twenty-five times a week. He never ate the food. He filled up on bread until he overdosed. Easy. I knew addiction ran in your family. Vito was gonna marry me at City Hall.

CHECKY: Auntie Pasto isn't gonna go for this.

CHEEKY: She's in on it with me. This is about enormous scale liberation.

CHECKY: But we're family. Cousins ten times removed.

CHEEKY: That means your people were colonizers to my people. And now we're taking everything back.

ESCAROLA: You'll never get pasta sold on the Black market.

CHEEKY: I'm not gonna sell it. I'm going to give it away to the people, like Robina Hood. Steal from the rich colonizers and give to the disenfranchised in city housing. It's always been about the elbows. Now I control the elbows. And controlling the elbows means my people and me control the macaroni and cheese. And then we're taking control over the collard greens and black-eyed peas.

ESCAROLA: Wait. That's not where my story ends. Vito was found naked walking across 125th Street at 5 AM, the morning of … What date is it? He had bulging belly bulimia. Eating, regurgitating, eating, regurgitating. You know the drill. Checky was arrested and given time served due to her broken heart. She moved overseas and became a bodyguard for spaghetti. Cheeky formed a new mob, Mac Mob. I'm Detective Escarola Bean Manicotti. My work never ends. Yes, Escarola Bean, and proud of it.

(Lights Out)

End of Play

Scars to Remember

Menses Dreams

Characters

Gram (Edna Mae): African American woman, eighty-something great grandmother

Cookie: African American, eighteen-year-old great granddaughter, fraternal twin

Cupcake: African American, eighteen-year-old great granddaughter, fraternal twin

Setting

The story begins in the family's two-story home. It is modest, clean, and filled with a few family treasures. Gram is in the kitchen ironing clothes. There is an ironing board, heavy iron, and a basket of clean laundry. Gram is singing a medley of her favorite Negro spirituals. Cookie and Cupcake are in the upstairs bedroom. The room is clean, neat, with two twin beds, a closet, desk, and chair. Cookie has her hands tied behind her back as she is seated on the chair. Cupcake is holding a hairbrush. She uses the end of the hairbrush to hit Cookie rapidly on the side of her head.

Lights Rise

COOKIE: Gram!

> (Cupcake holds her hand over Cookie's mouth as she continues to hit her head with the hairbrush.)

GRAM: Cookie, Cupcake…everything okay? It sounds so noisy up there.

CUPCAKE: Everything is fine Gram. It's not noisy. Just take off your hearing aid and adjust the volume control.

GRAM: (Removes her hearing aid and adjusts the setting) Oh, all right.

CUPCAKE: If you keep your mouth shut I'll take off this strap.

(Cookie indicates her agreement by nodding her head.
Cupcake puts down the hairbrush and begins to loosen the strap secured on Cookie's hands.)

GRAM: Yes, this is so much better. I always forget that I have a hearing aid in my bad ear. Had a hearing aid in my bad ear so long, it feels natural.

(Cookie gets up from the chair, knocks Cupcake to the floor, and sits on Cupcake bouncing up and down as she hits Cupcake with the end of the hairbrush. Cupcake screams from the pain. Plaster from the ceiling falls down into the kitchen where Gram is ironing the laundry. Gram looks up as the plaster falls down.)

COOKIE: How do you like it? Little knocks upside your head. Now we have matching bumps. Maybe they'll call us the head-bump twins? No, we can't have that. I'll need to give you a bigger bump.

(Cookie uses the end of the hairbrush to hit Cupcake with a rigorous blow. Cupcake screams.)

CUPCAKE: Gram!

(Cookie puts her hand over Cupcake's mouth.)

GRAM: I told that handyman that he needed to do more patching to the ceiling before he painted. All that plaster still falling down. I hear some noise upstairs.

COOKIE: If you want me to stop reshaping your head you need to stop screaming.

(Cupcake stops screaming. Cookie removes her hand from Cupcake's mouth.)

COOKIE: It's Okay Gram, we're playing a video game.

GRAM: Cookie, Cupcake, you have a big day tomorrow. You need to turn that television and that game off so you'll be fresh in the morning. And you know they said on the news that those video games make many children behave violently. Not a good thing to watch too much of those video games.

COOKIE & CUPCAKE: Yes Gram.

(Cupcake pushes her way up from the floor. Cookie feels her head. She is bleeding from one of the hairbrush blows.)

COOKIE: You broke the skin. I'm gonna have a scar.

CUPCAKE: Broke the skin. I shoulda broke more than that. I'll show you "broke."

(Cupcake goes to the closet. She throws a high heel shoe and hits Cookie.)

GRAM: Great-grandmother raising great-grandchildren. Time was when you were raising children you just had to think about normal things…the children being clean, getting an education, going to church, having nice friends, being polite. Nowadays have to think about video games and violence. Mercy…so thankful my great-granddaughters are not violent.

(Cookie throws the shoe back at Cupcake.)

COOKIE: You can keep your Gucci knock offs.

(GRAM takes two white blouses out of the laundry basket.)

GRAM: Cookie, Cupcake…I'm putting a little starch in your white blouses. Fixing them up nice for your big day.

COOKIE & CUPCAKE: Thanks Gram.

GRAM: My great-grandgirls are gonna have their big day. Playing duet piana in the concert hall downtown. Had a big day for myself once. EDNA MAE'S BIG DAY.

COOKIE: It was an accident. I was running for the bus, and I tripped on the sidewalk. Scraped up my ankle too. I got a scar on my heel.

(Cupcake goes to the closet. She holds up a handbag with a broken handle.)

CUPCAKE: What about this? Broke.

COOKIE: Did you expect me to use the knock off shoes without the knock off handbag?

CUPCAKE: I expect you to not use my stuff. I expect you to ask to borrow my things and not just take them.

COOKIE: I put too many things in the bag, and it was a little heavy. Cheap handle broke. Let's talk about ripped. (Picks up a dress from the bed and points out the rips in several places) Ripped, ripped, ripped, ripped.

GRAM: White gloves, white skirts, and white patent leather shoes. My skirt had a wide crinoline. My skirt stood out like a sculpture and moved and swirled like it was talking with every step I walked. On stage, getting my award my skirt was going to perform.

CUPCAKE: I was trying it on, and the seams popped. I was gonna sew the seams back.

COOKIE: Trying it on. You knew you couldn't fit this dress, fatty. I was gonna wear this after the concert today. Now what am I supposed to wear?

CUPCAKE: Something else. You have more clothes than me.

GRAM: My starched white blouse had a Peter Pan collar with little pearl buttons coming down the front. I remember watching my mother sew those buttons on one by one, sewing a little bit of herself with every loop of thread...wishing me luck... A big day for one person in the family was a big day for everyone in the family. That's the way things were for most back then. Everyone was so proud. Honor society. First time a girl from our side of the dirt—was in the honor society.

(Gram places the iron on the ironing board and practices walking across a stage, looking at an audience, and saying thank you for the honor.)

COOKIE: You mean you don't have any cute clothes. Gram gives you the same allowance. You can't fit the cute clothes, fatty.

GRAM: I'm so deeply thankful for the privilege of induction into the Colored Honor Society of Bridgehampton County, Virginia. I will always conduct myself with the respect and honor that is my responsibility as a representative of all of the colored high schools in Bridgehampton. Each girl would be dressed in white and have a certificate placed into her white gloved hand. It would be so beautiful.

CUPCAKE: Let me take a look at what I did. (Picks up the dress)

Did I rip it that badly? (Pulls the dress completely apart and then throws the dress at COOKIE) Now it's ripped badly.

GRAM: Why did it have to come that day? Why now… on my big day?

(Gram continues to iron. Cupcake and Cookie flip the mattresses of their twin beds on the sides using the mattresses as shields as they proceed to throw objects at each other. They reach and throw objects in the room as quickly as they can grab them. The fight continues as Gram is talking and ironing. Cupcake and Cookie are screaming at each other as they battle with objects in the room.)

GRAM: I always used clean rags wrapped up tight. Wrapped over and over and then secured the old panties with safety pins to the front and the back of the rags. It's what we did, the pads were too expensive. I was already dressed in the required white clothes. Mama pulled out a dollar from her ironing work jar and gave it to me. I needed a real pad just to be safe. If there was blood…while I was on stage… even a drop… I put my good shoes in a croaker sack and walked down the dirt road barefoot to Mr. Neiley's store. I had just enough time to get to the bus. Mrs. Aikens had said, "Don't be late for the bus. The ceremony is at ten o'clock. We have to get there ready to line up with all the other schools. You don't want to get left behind." I ran into the store out of breath. "Got any ladies pads Mr. Neily?"

CUPCAKE: This is the last time you're gonna take my shoes and bags without asking.

COOKIE: If I asked, you would you have said "yes"?

CUPCAKE: No.

GRAM: No colored allowed. There weren't signs: "FOR COLORED " and "FOR WHITES ONLY" on the

26

store because everyone knew nothing in this part of town were shared with the colored people.

COOKIE: You never want to share your stuff, but you think you should take my clothes. Why should I share my clothes that aren't going to fit you?

CUPCAKE: Why should I share with you if you're not gonna share with me? You're selfish.

GRAM: "Please sir…may I have a lady's napkin? I have money." He was mopping the floor of the store. He looked up at me as if he was looking at a monster…a dreadful, ugly monster. "Gal you know better, what you doing in this store?" Ain't no coloreds to be in here. "Please sir, it's important, I need a lady's napkin." He picked up the scrub brush for the floor and threw it at my head. Those sharp bristles cut me clear across my forehead. "Get out." I fell to the ground.

(Gram picks up the iron to continue pressing the blouses, and she places it on her opposite hand.)

COOKIE: Get out of my room.

CUPCAKE: It's not your room.

COOKIE: It is now.

(Cookie uses her mattress to push Cupcake toward the door of the bedroom. Cupcake resists.)

GRAM: The blood and the tears were so mixed up I couldn't see. Then I felt what I couldn't see. That man picked up that pail with the dirty water and threw it on me. My big day, my big…

(The heat of the iron burns Gram's hand. Gram faints. The iron, the ironing board, and the laundry fall to the kitchen floor.)

CUPCAKE & COOKIE: Gram!

(Cupcake and Cookie push the mattress aside and run down the stairs. Each trying to outrun the other.)

CUPCAKE & COOKIE: Gram. Gram.

(Cupcake and Cookie work together to revive Gram. They remove all the items around her, support her head with pillows, cover her with a sheet, get her a glass of water, put smelling salts under her nose, and clean and bandage her burn.)

CUPCAKE & COOKIE: Gram, Gram…

GRAM: Did I miss your big day?

CUPCAKE & COOKIE: No Gram.

GRAM: That's good.

CUPCAKE: You burned your hand on the iron, and you fainted.

GRAM: What about your white blouses?

COOKIE: (Picks up the blouses from the laundry) One is a little bit ruined Gram.

CUPCAKE: We'll figure out what to do. (Shows Gram her hand) The burn may leave a scar.

GRAM: I've gotten scars before. My scars help me remember my blessings. Your big day… I didn't miss your big day.

COOKIE: Yes, Gram we have a big day.

CUPCAKE: Big day.

(Family embrace)

(Lights Out)

End of Play

Doll Madness

Play Date

Characters

Alec: Male customer service representative

Janet Burns: Female customer

G.I. Joe: Life-size, adult doll. He's dressed in fatigues, combat helmet, and boots.

He has weapons.

New Edition Barbie: Life-size, adult Barbie doll. She has multicolored short hair, multiple body piercings, and "grunge" clothing.

T-Model Barbie: Life-size, adult Barbie doll. She's tall, slender with a large bosom and long hair. She's dressed in skinny jeans, a midriff top and high heel shoes.

Setting

Present day, in the customer service area of an Adult Toys R Us store. Alec stands behind the counter with a cash register/computer. G.I. Joe stands in combat readiness in front of the counter. T-Model Barbie stands opposite Alec behind the counter. Janet enters.

Lights Rise

ALEC: Welcome to Adult Toys R Us. May I help you?

JANET: I need to return a Barbie doll.

ALEC: (Entering notes into the computer) Not a problem. Let's start with your name first.

JANET: Janet Burns.

ALEC: And may I call you Janet during this transaction?

JANET: Yes.

ALEC: Awesome. And will you consent to complete a brief survey at the end of this transaction insuring that Adult Toys R Us has provided you with the best possible service today?

JANET: This is an emergency.

ALEC: Not a problem. One minute...(Alec types.)... ready...(Alec stops typing.)

Do you have the original box?

JANET: No. She was a gift shipped to my house. As soon as she arrived, she cut through the box with a razor blade and then shredded all the cardboard.

ALEC: (Types) Unusual.

JANET: Everything about her is unusual.

ALEC: Do you have the tags that were on the doll?

JANET: She cut them off and flushed them down the toilet.

ALEC: Not a problem. I can do a price check from her serial number. (Pause) I'll just need to take a look at the gift receipt.

JANET: I don't have a receipt. I told all my friends that I wanted an adult Barbie doll for my birthday. There wasn't a card or a gift receipt. Any one of my "friends" could have sent her. No one's claiming responsibility, so I think I've been pranked.

ALEC: I'm sorry, Janet. This return is going to be a little difficult.

JANET: You have to take her back. I can't just throw her away. She's dangerous. She can hurt somebody.

ALEC: Barbie is our most popular doll. I've never heard complaints that a Barbie doll was dangerous.

JANET: I'm afraid of her.

ALEC: Let me see what I can do. I need to make sure she's in resale condition.

JANET: She's outside.

ALEC: Bring her in please.

JANET: She's angry. She refused to come into the store. She doesn't want to be returned.

ALEC: There's nothing I can do if she's not in the store.

JANET: Okay. (Exiting) This will take a few minutes.

(Sound Effects: Items crashing, glass breaking, Janet screaming)

(Enter Janet, pulling New Edition Barbie resisting violently. Janet is in disarray and is exhausted.)

NEW EDITION BARBIE: You lying mother fu...

JANET: Fudge

NEW EDITION BARBIE: I knew you were taking me back to this fu...

JANET: Fudge

NEW EDITION BARBIE: Store. Who the fu...

JANET: Fudge

NEW EDITION BARBIE: are you?

JANET: BARBIE! I told you, don't use that foul language. It's vulgar.

NEW EDITION BARBIE: You're a mother fudger. I want to go home. Get me out of this fudge hole before somebody gets fudged up.

ALEC: Sometimes changes in the home environment can result in an upset Barbie. Any changes you can think of?

JANET: She arrived this way…aggressive…fighting…

ALEC: Have you considered bringing a Ken doll into your home for her companion?

JANET: I have a Ken doll. She hates him. She beats him up.

T-MODEL BARBIE: Ken is my boyfriend. I love him. We'll never get married. We'll be boyfriend and girlfriend forever and ever.

NEW EDITION BARBIE: He touched me.

JANET: He's supposed to touch you, Barbie. You're companions.

NEW EDITION BARBIE: Nobody can put hands on me without my permission.

T-MODEL BARBIE: I like to be touched.

ALEC: Sometimes when a Barbie can't adjust, we have to re-home her.

T-MODEL BARBIE: I have a home. I'm the T-Model Deluxe Barbie. I come with a condo and a pink convertible sports car. Let's go shopping first. Are you hungry? We can stop by my Barbie condo and have beverages and appetizers by the Barbie pool. I don't know how to cook, but I can order take out.

JANET: I want that Barbie.

ALEC: Let's do an even exchange.

T-MODEL BARBIE: I'll get my handbag and matching luggage.

NEW EDITION BARBIE: This is so fudged up.

ALEC: I need to examine your return and find the serial number.

NEW EDITION BARBIE: You want him to put his hands on me, Janet?

JANET: He won't hurt you, Barbie.

T-MODEL BARBIE: You can put your hands on me. I'll show you my numbers: 36-22-36.

ALEC: I don't want to upset her anymore. I'll find the serial number by the shipping date.

JANET: Barbie, please stand next to G.I. Joe.

NEW EDITION BARBIE: (Standing next to G.I. Joe) Nice fatigues and gear, soldier.

G.I. JOE: Thank you Ma'am.

NEW EDITION BARBIE: What's your mission here?

G.I. JOE: Protect and defend the Barbie dolls.

NEW EDITION BARBIE: Who's your commanding officer?

G.I. JOE: Mattel the Toy Maker, Ma'am.

NEW EDITION BARBIE: I want to talk to Mattel.

G.I. JOE: Unavailable, Ma'am.

NEW EDITION BARBIE: So you're on a mission to protect Barbie dolls, and your commanding officer isn't here. You're on your own soldier.

G.I. JOE: Ma'am?

NEW EDITION BARBIE: I'm a Barbie doll, and I need protection. And that T-Model Barbie over there is being held captive.

G.I. JOE: (Looking at T-Model Barbie) She's smiling.

NEW EDITION BARBIE: She's in shock. I've been kidnapped from my home. Adult Toys R Us is an international doll-trafficking criminal organization.

T-MODEL BARBIE: Is there time to change my outfit? I'd like to wear my pink empire dress with the coordinated coat and pillbox hat.

NEW EDITION BARBIE: Mattel the Toy Maker is compromised or gone. You have to save us!

G.I. JOE: Ma'am, yes Ma'am. Protect and defend the Barbie dolls.

ALEC: Here's the problem. Your New Edition Barbie is part of the limited release "Free Choice" line. We expected this design of Barbie dolls to be popular, but customers preferred the traditional models. You have one of the few of this model still left in circulation.

JANET: I want the T-Model. I wanted an adult Barbie doll to help me learn how to be perfect and alluring. What can I learn from that New Edition—nothing.

T-MODEL BARBIE: I'm pretty and alluring. Ken loves me.

NEW EDITION BARBIE: What kind of wheels do you have, soldier?

G.I. JOE: Jeep, tank, and helicopter, Ma'am.

NEW EDITION BARBIE: We should take the Barbie pink sports car…we'll attract less attention.

G.I. JOE: (Giving handgun to New Edition Barbie) Take my standard issue semi-automatic pistol Ma'am.

NEW EDITION BARBIE: Yeah, and give me a few of those hand grenades.

G.I. JOE: Cover me.

NEW EDITION BARBIE: (Firing the handgun into the air) Stay where you are. Hands in the air.

ALEC: Calm down. You don't need to do this.

JANET: I told you she was dangerous.

T-MODEL BARBIE: (Raising hands) Should I put my handbag down?

NEW EDITION BARBIE: Not you, Barbie...you're coming with us.

G.I. JOE: (Walking behind counter to get T-Model Barbie) Don't worry, Ma'am. I'm here to protect you.

T-MODEL BARBIE: I love men in uniforms. I wish Ken had a uniform. Would you get my luggage please, Soldier Joe?

(T-Model Barbie and G.I. Joe move towards the door.)

JANET: Don't take her. Come home with me. We'll go shopping. We can do hair and make-up. We can change outfits all day! What about Ken?

NEW EDITION BARBIE: You're free now, You can love whomever you want.

T-MODEL BARBIE: I love Ken. I love Joe. Joe has a uniform.

(T-Model Barbie and G.I. Joe exit.)

ALEC: Where will you go? What will you do?

NEW EDITION BARBIE: It doesn't matter. We're free. This is all your fault, Janet. All I wanted to do was love you.

(Exit New Edition Barbie.)

ALEC: I'll need to charge you for two additional dolls.

(Lights Out)

End of Play

Entonces Vivamos

Then We Live

Characters

MARTA CUEVAS: Gabriel's mother, Fernando's wife

FERNANDO CUEVAS: Gabriel's father, Marta's husband

GABRIEL CUEVAS: Fernando and Marta's deceased son

Setting

Present day, Bronx, New York City inside the family's two-bedroom apartment. Marta and Fernando prepare food on opposite sides of the large eat-in kitchen. Gabriel is seated at the table in the center of the room looking at a comic book and eating a bowl of rice with a spoon. Fernando looks inside the refrigerator.

Lights Rise

FERNANDO: Marta, Did you buy two bunches of cilantro?

MARTA: Si.

FERNANDO: I only see one bunch.

MARTA: Look on the top shelf, Fernando.

FERNANDO: Nada.

MARTA: Look in the vegetable drawer.

FERNANDO: Nada.

MARTA: Look under the packages of romaine lettuce in the corner behind the chorizo on the bottom shelf near the broken part.

FERNANDO: Nada.

MARTA: You're not looking with both eyes. Get your eyeglasses.

FERNANDO: Por favor Marta, will you come here and look for yourself?

MARTA: No…I'm busy. I have my own work.

FERNANDO: Madre de Dios.

(Fernando puts on his eyeglasses. He grabs bunches of herbs from the refrigerator and throws them where Marta is preparing food as he identifies each one.)

FERNANDO: Oregano, tomillo, albahaca, romero, estragon, perejil, chepil, hierbabuena (Holding up the bunch of cilantro and waving it at Marta) y solamente uno cilantro.

(Marta turns around and looks at Fernando. She wipes her hands on her apron and walks slowly and sensually towards Fernando. She takes Fernando's hand holding the cilantro and places it next to his lips. She takes a bite of the leaves.)

MARTA: Yes, this is cilantro…and it is very fresh… very tender…very fragrant…

(Marta removes the cilantro from Fernando's hand and places it on the counter where she is working. Marta gathers all of the herbs thrown on her side of the kitchen and places them where Fernando is preparing food.)

MARTA: Your side…my side… Stay on your side.

FERNANDO: I'm happy to stay on the side where I can have peace.

(Marta smells the cilantro and separates the sprigs of the bunch. She looks through the kitchen drawers taking out utensils.)

MARTA: Where is the good knife?

FERNANDO: What do you mean, "the good knife"?

MARTA: You know what I mean, Fernando…the good knife.

FERNANDO: Every knife in this kitchen is good. Did you look on your side?

MARTA: It's not here.

FERNANDO: Use another knife from your side of the kitchen.

MARTA: Another knife? I want the knife my great-grandmother held in her mouth when she swam across the river to escape persecution with my grandmother tied to her back. I want the knife my great-grandmother passed down to grandmother that she used to prepare the first meal for the family in America. I want the knife that my grandmother gave my mother on her wedding day wrapped in the apron that my grandmother wore when she prepared the first meal for the family in America. I want the knife my mother passed down to me for my first kitchen to use to prepare food for my family with the blessing that we should never be hungry and that God-willing should I ever have a child I should give that knife to my son or my daughter to use in their kitchen so the food will be cut and prepared with the love and sacrifices of generations with every cut. I want that good knife.

FERNANDO: Did you look under your pillow? I think that's the same knife you use to cut my heart out before I sleep at night.

(Marta opens a kitchen drawer and takes out a knife. She throws it at the wall above the stove.)

MARTA: No…that is the knife for your heart. I always forget to take it out of the kitchen drawer and put it under my pillow. That is why you wake up alive every morning, mi amor.

FERNANDO: Marta, my sweet… Please remind me to sharpen your knives. My heart has grown cold and hard during our marriage. You will need a much sharper knife if you want to cut out my heart.

(They throw kisses. Fernando gets "the good knife.")

FERNANDO: This is the knife you want.

MARTA: Si… This is the knife. Gracias.

FERNANDO: I was thinking…

MARTA: For once in our marriage you were thinking?

FERNANDO: Since we met, Marta…there's been a problem with my thinking. When I decided to ask for your hand…

MARTA: The day Uncle Tito threatened to hide me in a convent…

FERNANDO: I was a nervous young man… My thinking told me, "Don't hesitate. This woman's soul and your soul belong together. You'll be happy."

MARTA: I said "yes" without delay. I believe I was under the spell of a bruja…

FERNANDO: Then I had the opportunity to change my decision again before our promise ceremony. And my thoughts tell me, "Yes…promise yourself to this woman. Two souls destined for each other have met."

MARTA: Yes, it must have been a spell…because I only remember feeling that my life needed completion with you.

FERNANDO: Then for the third time when I stood on the steps of the church en Cordoba where my great-grandparents, and my grandparents, and my parents were wed… And I think again. And my thoughts say meet Marta inside the church and marry her.

Since I followed my thinking and I married you… I decided never again will I think while this woman is in my life.

MARTA: I told you we should get married in the Bronx.

FERNANDO: But this time, my sweet, my thinking is not flawed… I'm preparing salsa verde for pork. Puerco Salsa Verde the way it was prepared for our promise ceremony.

MARTA: This is Gabriel's birthday. How could you do this to me? For seventeen years we prepared Tia Lupita's recipe for Arroz Verde for him.

FERNANDO: This year will be different.

MARTA: You insult Gabriel's memory. Arroz Verde.

FERNANDO: Gabriel hated rice.

(Marta takes the good knife and holds it up to Fernando face.)

MARTA: Take the knife to my neck. I'm already dead from your words.

FERNANDO: When Gabriel was a child, you forced him to eat the rice, and he obeyed. When he became a man he ate the rice out of love and respect for you but then, after dinner, he went to the diner and ate hot dogs and greasy French fries with ketchup.

41

MARTA: He was never a man.

FERNANDO: I'm going to prepare my family's recipe brought from Ecuador, brought to Argentina, brought to the Bronx.

MARTA: He was never a man.

FERNANDO: I need the cilantro, to make some fresh cilantro for the salsa verde.

MARTA: He was never a man.

FERNANDO: Give me the cilantro, Marta. Since there's only one bunch if you insist on preparing green rice, you'll have to make the green rice with something else green, not cilantro.

MARTA: He was a seventeen-year-old child.

FERNANDO: Madre de Dios. Marta, give me the cilantro. I just want a change.

MARTA: No cambio.

FERNANDO: No es importante.

MARTA: Yes, it is important. I see him at the table with his favorite bowl…and his favorite spoon. A Chinese soupspoon…to eat Mexican rice. He always ate so strange. He mixed the chorizo and the pollo in small pieces into the rice.

GABRIEL: Delicioso Mom.

FERNANDO: Gabriel ate the rice because he loved you, and when he ate the rice, he knew it pleased you.

MARTA: Fernando, for once in our marriage you're right. Your heart has grown cold and hard. Es impossible para mi cut out your heart, but you, mi amor, have successfully cut out mine.

FERNANDO: No hay problema. Make the rice our dead son hated.

MARTA: I know he hated the rice. I told him, "You don't need to eat the rice Gabriel. I make it only for tradition." But he insisted on eating it…his special way with the chorizo and the pollo he enjoyed. I made the rice, he ate the rice to say…

GABRIEL: I love you Mom.

FERNANDO: We need to eat the food that will remind us of our love for each other.

MARTA: You took my son from me. I don't know that I can ever love you the same.

FERNANDO: He was *our* son Marta, and he was a young man.

MARTA: He was a child, and you helped kill him.

FERNANDO: Adulto…We married when we were seventeen.

MARTA: It was a different time. It was a different place. We had seen so much about life already when we were seventeen. His life was supposed to be different.

FERNANDO: He told me…

GABRIEL: Mom will never give me permission to enlist. I only need one parent's signature.

MARTA: He asked us first together before I left for Mexico. We agreed together. We told him no. "There's no need to do this now…you're seventeen…you have time for a decision that will change your life." *We* were his parents. You broke the decision *we* made.

FERNANDO: He came into the house late. He knew I would be waiting up. He showed me the recruitment brochures.

GABRIEL: Mira Pa...Cada soldado tiene sus razones peronales para unrise al U.S. Army, y su hijo o su hija no es differente...

FERNANDO: He wanted me to watch the recruitment videos, and then...

Bastante Gabriel. I don't need these brochures and videos. I don't need to know what these soldiers and their families think. You're from a people who know the price of freedom, who know what it means to protect and defend...but you have choices. We've worked hard. *We have money for your college.* (Pause) What is it? You don't want to go to college now? Okay. What do you want to do? You don't have to work in the restaurant. Tell me what you want. We can figure this out.

GABRIEL: (Placing the documents on the table) I want to be a soldier.

FERNANDO: There's time...You don't need to make a decision now that can change your life forever.

GABRIEL: The right time is a decision between me and God. Pa, Yo soy un hombre. No man can tell another man how to follow his soul. Let me follow my soul. It's my right. Pa...por favor.

FERNANDO: Gabriel! (Pause) Be reasonable.

GABRIEL: Pa...I'm just a regular guy, and I've had enough of being regular. I can be a great soldier. I've been protecting something or somebody since I was a little kid.

(Pause)

Do you remember the pregnant dog that gave birth on abuela's porch?

FERNANDO: No one in the family will forget that dog or you…twelve years old…pulling a pregnant dog in a makeshift wagon across Fordham Road.

GABRIEL: Hit and run of a dog. That coward cab driver just drove off. If I didn't bring the dog home, the mother and the puppies would have died.

FERNANDO: The mother did die.

GABRIEL: She lived long enough to give birth and nurse her puppies for a few days. Don't you remember? The puppies lived, and I found homes for all five.

FERNANDO: Do you remember how many days you cried after the mother died? No one could comfort you.

GABRIEL: I'm not twelve years old anymore.

FERNANDO: But we're not talking about puppies either. In war, we're talking about people dying, and we're talking about you…

GABRIEL: I saw Eddie Rodriguez yesterday.

FERNANDO: Chubs?

GABRIEL: The one and only. He still remembers when I protected him from Miguel in sixth grade. Do remember what you said to me?

FERNANDO: That has nothing to do with now. Sixth graders weren't in gangs then bringing guns and knives to playgrounds.

GABRIEL: You told me I should help Eddie if he was being bullied by talking first and making peace. But if I had to hit Miguel, hit him as hard as I could and make it count. Miguel never picked on Eddie again. I was a peacemaker. That's the kind of soldier I'll be…a peacemaker.

FERNANDO: (Indicates information on the documents) The start date on these enlistment papers is one week after your graduation.

GABRIEL: (Picks up the documents from the table) Yes, Pa… my graduation gift.

(Fernando reaches out and takes the documents from Gabriel. Gabriel puts on an army uniform and combat hat that is hanging on the back of the chair. He salutes. He leaves the kitchen and exits the front door to the battlefield.)

GABRIEL: Private Gabriel Cuevas reporting for duty, Sir.

MARTA: When did God make the decision that sons should die before their mothers?

FERNANDO: In thirty-five years of marriage, I had never kept a secret from you. I had never broken a promise to you. I'm so sorry. I'm so very sorry.

(Marta takes sprigs of cilantro and places them in Fernando's hand. She takes a few leaves and chews them as she looks at Fernando. She places a few leaves in his mouth, and he chews them. Fernando turns on Tango music played at their wedding: Desde el Alma.

Marta removes her apron. Fernando offers his hand to Marta. They dance their wedding dance in the kitchen. The dance ends in front of the door.)

MARTA: Sometimes God plays tricks on mothers. We think we are giving birth to a child, but we give birth to a man. Gabriel decided when he wanted to be born. Do you remember? Almost two weeks late.

FERNANDO: Lo recuerdo.

MARTA: Did he decide it might be his time to die and he didn't want to tell me? If I understood his passion to be a soldier I wouldn't have stood in the way.

GABRIEL: (Writing a letter) Dear Mom and Pa

MARTA: He didn't trust me. You had the burden of protection of his soul by yourself. I'm sorry, Fernando. I'm sorry, Gabriel.

(Gabriel places his rifle and bayonet in ready position. SOUND EFFECTS: bombs, small firearms, artillery, shouts of commands from officers)

GABRIEL: Kabul feels like the furthest place on earth from the Bronx. I think of you every day, but I try not to. When you're distracted, that's when things happen. I'm going to miss my eighteenth birthday with you. Do something for me…make coconut cake. Put eighteen candles on it, then another one for good luck. Blow out the candles and think of me.

Te amo.

FERNANDO: It's time.

MARTA: It's time.

(Black out on Gabriel. Lights in kitchen fade to dim. Marta takes a birthday cake out of the refrigerator and places it on the kitchen table. Fernando gets candles from the kitchen cabinet. They decorate the cake with the candles. Marta places a framed photograph of Gabriel on the table. Marta and Fernando hold hands and sing a "Happy Birthday" song in Spanish.)

MARTA & FERNANDO: May the souls of the faithful departed through the mercy of God rest in peace.

(Lights rise on Gabriel as he enters the kitchen. Marta and Fernando blow out all of the candles on the cake except one. GABRIEL blows out the remaining candle.)

(Lights Out)

End of Play

Note: Desde el Alma *by Rosita Melo, circa 1911*

Style by Design

Suitable

Characters

Mr. Henry: Handsome, African American man, impeccably dressed in business attire, middle-aged, men's stylist Viktor Caldwell: Handsome, nineteen, African American man, dressed in oversized jeans, sleeveless T-shirt, and trendy sneakers

Setting

The interior of Style by Design, a men's fashion store on 125th Street in Harlem. Viktor enters from the front door facing the street. The door chime rings. Mr. Henry enters from the rear of the store from behind drapes. A table and two chairs are in the center of the store. The interior of the store is filled with a few racks of sample clothing, photographs of celebrities with Mr. Henry, fashion awards Mr. Henry has achieved, and a full-size mirror.

Lights Rise

MR. HENRY: Good Afternoon. May I help you?

VIKTOR: I need a shirt and a pair of pants that match. I have some place important to go.

MR. HENRY: I'm sorry, you must have the wrong address.

(Viktor takes a piece of paper out of one pocket of his jeans and looks at it while he uses his other hand to hold up his jeans, which will fall below his rear unless secured.)

VIKTOR: Mr. Henry. I need a shirt and a pair of pants that match. I have to go to somethin important.

MR. HENRY: How old are you, Son?

VIKTOR: Nineteen.

MR. HENRY: Do you remember when you were in kindergarten and your teacher asked you to choose things that went together like shapes and colors?

VIKTOR: Yeah.

MR. HENRY: That's called matching. This is a business where we coordinate apparel for men. We don't match shirts and pants. If you need some matching clothing there are several places along 125th where you can go from rack to rack and match shirts and pants to your heart's content.

(Viktor removes a black envelope with a gold seal from his pocket and offers it to Mr. Henry. Mr. Henry views the envelope.)

VIKTOR: Here.

MR. HENRY: A gold-seal referral. I only give these to my favorite clientele, and each client only receives one each year. You're special to someone.

(Mr. Henry sits down and puts on his reading eyeglasses. He opens the envelope and reviews the referral.)

VIKTOR: My unk told me to give you the envelope if you weren't gonna help me.

MR. HENRY: Luther Caldwell is your uncle? Archie Caldwell is your father?

VIKTOR: Yeah.

MR. HENRY: Have a seat.

VIKTOR: Measure me up and give me the clothes.

MR. HENRY: (Walking toward the rear of the store) Off the rack…matching…down the street….east and west sides of 125th street.

VIKTOR: He told me to give you this note if you started to walk away. It's hand-written from my unk. It has a check.

MR. HENRY: (Reading the letter) *"Dear Mr. Henry, Here is an additional fee for your trouble. I didn't explain your procedures to my nephew. I thought it would be best if you did that yourself."*

Your uncle is an exceptional person. I have a great deal of respect for him. Why didn't your father write a note on your behalf?

VIKTOR: (Sits) What do I have to do? I want to get goin.

MR. HENRY: The initial consultation is approximately three hours. Then you'll come back for the secondary meeting after I work up a schematic of your body shape, and I'll propose some styling based on the information from your responses on my questionnaire.

VIKTOR: Did you hear me? I have somewhere to go and somethin important to do. It's tomorrow. Give me somethin from these racks. You must have my size.

MR. HENRY: (Gets up from his chair and prepares to leave the showroom) It doesn't work like that. I'll give my personal regrets to your uncle.

VIKTOR: (Reaches into his jean pocket. The pocket is bulging in the shape of a handgun.) Stop. Don't make me use this. I don't want to use this.

(Mr. Henry stops, and places his hands into the air as Viktor moves slowly towards him. VIKTOR stops and slowly moves a bulky document from his pocket and hands it to Mr. Henry. Mr. Henry takes the document slowly.)

MR. HENRY: A notarized petition requesting my assistance? How many names are on here? Your Cousin Sherice, your Uncle Bobby, your sister April, your Aunt Lucy, your Grandmother Kate, your play cousin…your play cousin?

VIKTOR: I'm here because I have to be here. Let's get to it.

MR. HENRY: Yes. Let's get to it.

MR. HENRY: (Placing documents on the table and writing) A man's image is his first statement to the world. A man's clothing begins a conversation before he says his first word. Your clothing gives the first "Hello," "Hi," and "What's up?" Your clothes look a woman in her eyes and smile. Your clothes confirm to a potential employer that you can represent the company and do the job. Perhaps your family wants you to start your non-verbal conversations a little differently? You gain entry or not with your appearance.

VIKTOR: I don't need the lecture.

MR. HENRY: (Looking at Viktor's clothing) No lecture. How are those clothes working for you? You're a man. Your clothing and how you wear your clothing is your choice. I'm simply going to help you through a process of intentional styling so you can make informed choices about your image…choose styles for the conversation you want to begin with others. You want your clothes to say I've arrived, I'm successful, and I'm ready to do it all.

Stand up please.

(Viktor rises from the chair. Mr. Henry begins measurements. Viktor's hand, which is holding up his shorts, is in the way.)

MR. HENRY: Hands at your sides please.

VIKTOR: I can't.

MR. HENRY: Step behind the drapes please.

(Viktor steps behind the drapes. His jeans fall to the floor. A paper bag falls out of his clothing. Viktor doesn't notice Mr. Henry picking up the bag.)

MR. HENRY: A little bit like performance art. You hold them in place. Pants up, pants down. (Takes measurements and then gives Viktor a belt from a display.) Just for the consultation and fitting…then you can continue your…

(Mr. Henry and Viktor sit at the consultation table. MR. HENRY takes notes.)

MR. HENRY: Let's talk about the garments you own so we can mix them up with some new pieces. Your family has been very generous with providing funds for your wardrobe, but let's stay within a reasonable budget. Let's make a list.

VIKTOR: I have a few hoodies, tees, Knick caps, some basketball shorts, and a few jeans.

MR. HENRY: Blazers? (Pause) Jackets?

VIKTOR: Leather.

MR. HENRY: Anything we might call shoes?

VIKTOR: Basketball shoes, some limited editions.

MR. HENRY: No shoes. (Balls up the questionnaire and throws it in the garbage) You have an assortment of undergarments, I'm assuming.

VIKTOR: Drawers?

MR. HENRY: I notice you've selected undergarments that lead the viewer's attention directly to your genitals, crotch and the crevice of your rear end. Is this where you choose to begin your conversations… from your penis, between your legs, and your anus?

VIKTOR: (Impatiently looks at his cell phone) I'm here because I have to be here.

MR. HENRY: Your family wants you fitted for a suit. The letter indicates you've agreed to cooperate. I'm simply making an observation. Viktor, a man designs his own style. This consultation and fitting is really about your choices. My question is, are you taking ownership of your power to design your life and your style, or have you given that power to someone else. Can you tell me about your reference?

VIKTOR: You mean like for a term paper?

MR. HENRY: Your reference. The inspiration for your style choices?

VIKTOR: It's just how we look.

MR. HENRY: We?

VIKTOR: My crew.

MR. HENRY: You're a follower then? It's your social tradition?

VIKTOR: It's not that deep. I dress the way I dress. I'm flipping my style for a minute so I can take care of somethin.

MR. HENRY: Actually, it is deep. I'll show you some examples of images that might be references for your choices, if not to you…to the people you encounter. (Brings photo journals to the consultation table) Men's undergarments are intended for comfort and to shape the fit of the pant on top. Since you're not concerned about fit, I question why you bother with undergarments at all? (Opens one book and points out some photographs.)

Here are some examples of people around the world who choose not to wear foundation garments or limit coverage of their genitals. I have some historical references, and here are some contemporary groups from the Amazon, Congo, and Papua New Guinea.

VIKTOR: Those people have nothin to do with me.

MR. HENRY: I understand the intentions of these people, and I respect their choices. Their choices are appropriate for their lifestyle. Your choices confuse me. Exposing your undergarments results in clear outlines of your anatomy…your genitals and your rear crevice. Are you making some statement about your male strength and assertiveness?

VIKTOR: Yeah. My male strength.

MR. HENRY: Why not make a bold, more confident statement then?

VIKTOR: I can feel that.

MR. HENRY: Wear boxers in a sheer fabric leaving less to the viewer's imagination, or forget the undergarments altogether, full exposure. Unless you leak from your orifices, full exposure shouldn't be a problem. Some effective treatments with scrubbing, exfoliation and a gentleman's Brazilian wax would do quite nicely to improve your appearance. Two quick rips with the hot wax strips, and all those little hairs in your butt crack will be cleanly lifted off.

VIKTOR: You're sick.

MR. HENRY: You'd prefer laser treatments? I've never tried it, but some of my transgender clients find it works well on dark, coarse hairs.

VIKTOR: Transgender? I'm straight.

MR. HENRY: Grooming is grooming. Prefer electrolysis? You're a manly man. You can manage an electric shock at the base of each hair follicle in your rear end. (Imitates the zap sound of the electrolysis gun) Removing one hair at a time. (Imitates the zap sound of the electrolysis gun) Remember to breathe when you feel the heat. I'll prepare a list of licensed practitioners in the Harlem area.

(Viktor paces the consultation area.)

MR. HENRY: You're upset. Is there a problem?

VIKTOR: Get me my apparel so I can get out of here.

MR. HENRY: Apparel? We're making progress. Let's just talk about shapes. Let's begin with where you are, and then let's find a reference that works for you as well as your family's requirements. (Turns to a page in a photo journal) Bozo the Clown. Bozo remains the international reference for clown attire. When I look at you, I feel an odd combination of an urge to laugh hysterically and weep at the tragedy. Bozo… definitely… I see several similarities: bright colors, voluminous shapes, and unstructured and oversized separates…a red wig and a red bubble nose, and we could pull your present image together nicely. How do you feel about white face and bold lip liner? Ready to move on?

VIKTOR: Move on.

MR. HENRY: Have a look at some of the photographs of well-tailored men on the walls while I pull out some ready to wear suits.

(Viktor looks at the photographs while Mr. Henry brings some suits from the back room.)

VIKTOR: These people really been in here, or are these pictures fake?

MR. HENRY: I won't answer that.

VIKTOR: (Focusing on a specific photograph) Now this is fresh. I could get some serious pus...

MR. HENRY: Yes, many ladies seem to like that look on a gentleman. I took the liberty to bring you somethin similar.

VIKTOR: (Viktor tries on a blazer and looks into the mirror) That's hard.

MR. HENRY: It's a little festive. You need somethin more subtle and conservative. (Helps Viktor with a second blazer) I suggest this navy blue pinstripe for your basic choice.

VIKTOR: I'll take the other one.

MR. HENRY: Why, son?

VIKTOR: I said I'll take the other one.

MR. HENRY: You look like your Dad.

VIKTOR: You don't know nothin about my Dad.

MR. HENRY: I know your Dad was a fine, hard-working gentleman who wore his clothing with pride and carried himself with pride. I tailored a suit like this for him.

VIKTOR: You've been settin me up. (Pulls a page from a newspaper from his pocket and reads) Archibald Caldwell, beloved husband of Sharon Caldwell, survived by daughter April and son Viktor, was killed in a drive-by shooting as he opened the front door of his home on 130th Street in Harlem. He was on his way to work. Police believe Mr. Caldwell was an innocent victim of perpetrators who intended the bullets for someone else. (Crushes the newspaper in his hand and lets it fall to the floor.) They were looking for me. Those bullets were intended for me. I'm wearing these clothes to his funeral. I'm carryin his casket.

MR. HENRY: I knew your father was murdered. I didn't know he took your bullets.

VIKTOR: Why were you sweatin me?

MR. HENRY: Clothes are not the most important part of being a man, son.

VIKTOR: Don't call me son. I'm nobody's son now.

MR. HENRY: You're still your father's son.

(Lights Out)

Lights Rise

VIKTOR: Why were you sweatin me?

MR. HENRY: Clothes are not the most important part of being a man, son.

VIKTOR: Don't call me son. I'm nobody's son now.

MR. HENRY: You're still your father's son.

VIKTOR: You have your money and you had your fun. Now give me my stuff on a hanger so I can get out of here and handle my business.

MR. HENRY: You're welcome. I'll hem your pants to the measurements, and you can be on your way.

VIKTOR: How long is that gonna take?

MR. HENRY: My measurements are precise, but I'll still want you to have a final fit after the alterations.

(Viktor exits toward the shop door.
Mr. Henry holds up Viktor's brown paper bag.)

MR. HENRY: You're going to need this. There's never a last deal, or a last hit. There's never going to be a payback that will bring your father back to life.

VIKTOR: (Lunges forward and takes the bag from Mr. Henry) This ain't nothin. I went soft for a minute. I shoulda hit first. (Pause) I'll be back in an hour for my apparel.

(Lights Out)

Lights Rise

VIKTOR: Why were you sweating me?

MR. HENRY: Clothes are not the most important part of being a man, son.

VIKTOR: Don't call me son. I'm nobody's son now.

MR. HENRY: You're still your father's son, and I'm still your father's friend.

VIKTOR: Stop with your lies old man. You think I'm a punk you can play twice?

MR. HENRY: "We have a choice." That's what your father said to me. We were your age. 130th Street… same street, different day…but it was our friend JT. No drive-by. No gun. Up close and personal with a shank. That was old school. We could follow JT into the grave, or we could give up the names of the thieves who stole his life. You have a choice Viktor.

(Lights Out)

(Sound Effect: Store window breaking. Gun shot. Screams in the darkness.)

VIKTOR: Mr. Henry. Mr. Henry?

(Lights Out)

End of Play

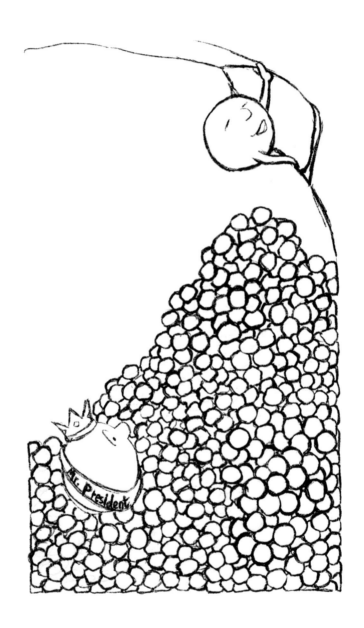

Frozen Stiffs

To Split or Not to Split

Characters

Marty: Executive Vice President Frozen Green Pea for Research & Development

Jake: Executive Vice President Frozen Green Pea for Accounting & Safety

Setting

The Bergman family home. Inside the bag of frozen green peas in the freezer section of the refrigerator.

Lights Rise

MARTY: How's your day so far Jake?

JAKE: Good. How's your day so far Marty?

MARTY: Good. Can't complain. Cold enough for you?

JAKE: Sure. Same as yesterday. Feels the same. Cold enough for you?

MARTY: Good. Can't complain. Maybe we should start work?

JAKE: Maybe. That's an idea.

MARTY: Start early, knock off early.

JAKE: Start early, knock off early. Sounds good.

MARTY: Good. And I was thinking maybe we should count the peas another way.

JAKE: Count another way? Why would we want to change from the way we always count the peas?

MARTY: Could be good. As Executive Vice President Frozen Green Pea in charge of Research & Development, it's my job to think of new ways to do our jobs.

JAKE: Makes a lot of sense Marty. Wait a minute. Counting is part of accounting. As the Executive Vice President Frozen Pea in charge of Accounting & Safety I should have been consulted.

MARTY: I'm consulting with you now. No decision's been made.

JAKE: You're right. You're right. I think we can consider a change.

MARTY: Thanks Jake. I appreciate your flexibility. By the way, we have counted the peas the same way since we were factory-sealed in this bag. How long have we been in here?

JAKE: I did think about that once. I did an estimation.

MARTY: Is that a fact?

JAKE: I was thinking at the time the accounting part of my job meant that I should count anything that could be counted. So I decided I should count the number of years this bag of green peas has been in the Bergman refrigerator freezer.

MARTY: Wait a minute, Jake. Sounds like that work is cutting pretty close to research. You should have consulted me.

JAKE: I'm consulting you now.

MARTY: And I appreciate that.

JAKE: Not a problem. Honestly, I didn't think about it at the time. We could always start again and work together. Two peas are better than one.

MARTY: Well, how far did you get.

JAKE: An estimation.

MARTY: You said that. What's the estimation?

JAKE: I did an estimate of the estimation. It's rough.

MARTY: Sure. Sure. I'll keep that in mind. A rough. Just a rough. A place to start from for further research.

JAKE: A rough.

MARTY: A rough.

JAKE: Twenty years.

MARTY: We've been in this freezer twenty years? That's your rough?

JAKE: Based on the facts as I know them, this bag of green peas has been in this freezer about two years "PF," post factory. No way to tell how long the bag was in the factory, then how long the bag was in the supermarket before the Bergman family purchased the bag and put us in this freezer.

MARTY: Post Factory…hum…would it help us if the expiration date was stamped on the inside of the bag instead of the outside?

JAKE: That would be an interesting accounting challenge. But it doesn't matter. Expiration dates are factory fiction.

MARTY: Tell me how you came up with the number.

JAKE: My estimation?

MARTY: Your estimation. How did you come up with the number?

JAKE: I don't have a problem sharing my formula. It's a rough.

MARTY: You said that already. It's a rough. It's a rough! What's the formula?

JAKE: I'm not sure I'm liking your tone Marty. This is the second refrigerator we've been in at the Bergman home.

MARTY: Seriously? I had no idea.

JAKE: The family kept the first refrigerator about ten years.

MARTY: How do you know it was ten?

JAKE: Their spending patterns. About every thirty days they put new packages in the freezer.

MARTY: How can you tell when there are more packages?

JAKE: Ever notice how sometimes the bag feels shoved around? That's when new packages get put in the freezer.

MARTY: Brilliant.

JAKE: Once a month this bag of peas gets shoved around for other food. That's twelve times a year. Hundred and twenty times makes ten years. You know the old saying, "Turn your bad peas into pea soup?"

MARTY: Can't say I heard that one Jake.

JAKE: I used to feel bad. I took it personal-like that the Bergmans wouldn't eat peas. Then I decided to use the information. Make the accounting work a little more interesting.

MARTY: You said twenty years.

JAKE: After ten years without leaving the freezer, the Bergmans purchased an energy efficient high-end upright modern freezer-fridge combo.

MARTY: Is that a fact?

JAKE: That's a fact.

MARTY: This isn't the freezer we originated in.

JAKE: Not the same.

MARTY: You've brought something very important to my attention. I need to be more observant.

JAKE: They took the bag out of the freezer for a few hours. The peas started to thaw.

MARTY: Come to think of it, I do remember some time back feeling a little warm.

JAKE: I thought we were finally going to get cooked. But they just wanted to transfer us to the new freezer. Then I started to count again. Thirty days a month. Twelve months a year. One hundred and twenty months. Ten years.

MARTY: Whew! I'm impressed.

JAKE: Thanks Marty. Mind a couple of questions about your estimation?

JAKE: Not at all. Shoot.

MARTY: How do you know when the day starts and ends?

JAKE: Interesting. Hadn't considered being precise with counting days.

MARTY: And, don't some months have thirty-one days?

JAKE: Hum. Right about that Marty.

MARTY: And…

JAKE: Whoa. You said a few questions. That means two. Three is optional when you say "a few" in accounting.

MARTY: Meant no disrespect.

JAKE: None taken.

MARTY: I'm very impressed with your estimation and the formula behind it.

JAKE: Thank you Marty. Means a lot to me, coming from you.

MARTY: And it fits in with my research.

JAKE: Interesting. What research is that?

MARTY: It's just a theory.

JAKE: I understand, just a theory.

MARTY: No hard evidence.

JAKE: Sometimes a theory is based on a hunch.

MARTY: I theorize that a bag of green peas can last forever in a freezer.

JAKE: Interesting. In twenty years not one green pea in this bag has disintegrated.

MARTY & JAKE: Interesting.

JAKE: Hey Marty, you suggested we start work early and knock off early. Still time to do that?

MARTY: We've been estimating and theorizing. We forgot we have our routine work to do!

JAKE: Marty, I say we plunge ahead and count your new way. Why not?

MARTY: Why not?

JAKE & MARTY: Why not?

MARTY: One of us starts the count at the top of the bag. The other one starts the count at the bottom of the bag. We meet in the middle and then add up the total number of peas. And…we count by two's.

JAKE: Really innovative. (Pause) Then we compare the number of peas from this inventory count to the number from the last inventory count.

MARTY: And when was that?

JAKE: I don't know since we don't know when the day starts and ends.

MARTY: And if my theory that frozen peas last forever is true, it doesn't matter.

JAKE & MARTY: Teamwork!

MARTY: I'll take the top.

JAKE: I guess I'll take the bottom. Go.

MARTY: What if there's an odd number? I hadn't considered that when I suggested we count by two's.

JAKE: There's always an even number of peas in a bag of frozen peas.

(Marty and Jake count the peas simultaneously aloud, loud and soft, brief periods of silent counting, repetitions, do-over's, all until they finish their sections of the bag. Then they mumble as they add their two numbers together.)

JAKE: Two thousand six hundred forty-two on the nose.

MARTY: Matches the last inventory total?

JAKE: That it does.

MARTY & JAKE: Teamwork!

JAKE: Hard day.

MARTY: Yes, hard day. Lots of innovations today.

JAKE: Lots of good innovations.

MARTY & JAKE: Teamwork!

JAKE: Marty?

MARTY: Something on your mind Jake.

JAKE: Have you ever considered the development part of your job as Vice President Frozen Green Pea for Research and **Development**?

MARTY: Can't say I've considered it.

JAKE: Then how do you know you're fulfilling all the responsibilities of your position?

MARTY: I think the development part of my position will just develop.

JAKE: That's interesting. Marty?

MARTY: Something else on your mind Jake?

JAKE: Actually I think I might have a safety issue we need to consider since we've recently been considering other considerations.

MARTY: And what might that be Jake?

JAKE: Something in consideration of the safety part of my position as Vice President Frozen Green Pea for accounting and **Safety.**

MARTY: Is that a fact?

JAKE: It's a fact. Remember when I was telling you about the bag getting pushed around to make room for other food packages.

MARTY: Actually, I do recall you mentioning that.

JAKE: Well, after one such rumble, a hole was ripped in the bag.

MARTY: Is that a fact?

JAKE: It's a fact. Top right corner.

(Jake and Marty look at the top right corner of the bag.)

MARTY: It's a hole. I can see it's a hole.

JAKE: I didn't bring the hole to your attention before, seeing as we didn't lose any peas, you know, falling through the hole. But at the moment it seems like a consideration that needs to be considered.

MARTY: What exactly is the consideration you think should be considered?

JAKE: One of us should look through the hole.

MARTY: You're talking about more work. I'm not sure I can go along on this idea.

JAKE: Just hear me out Marty.

MARTY: We have been considering some new considerations today. Maybe it's time to consider another consideration.

JAKE: What if I were to climb up and look out of the hole?

MARTY: Awe, I don't know about that. This here sounds like a new procedure. The president would have to be consulted.

JAKE: Is there a president?

MARTY: Every bag of frozen green peas has a president.

JAKE: If we are executive vice presidents and there must be a president, how come I've never seen him?

MARTY: Me neither. Maybe at the frozen pea factory they forgot to assign a president for this bag.

JAKE: Seeing as this has been kinda sorta a democracy, and seeing as we've been working as a team, I suggest we elect a president.

MARTY: Elect a president?

JAKE: An **executive** vice president to help make executive decisions.

MARTY: Sounds like a plan, but each of us already has a job as an executive **vice** president.

JAKE: Let's take a vote and see how it turns out. Maybe the president will want to consider the jobs a little differently. Let's do a simple, "Yay" vote.

MARTY: Sounds like a plan. You go ahead and manage the election. You came up with the idea.

JAKE: Okay then. All those who want to elect Jake president say, "Yay." That would be zero.

JAKE: All those who want to elect Marty president say, "Yay."

JAKE & MARTY: Yay

JAKE: That would be zero for me and two for you, Marty. You win the election by a landslide. Congratulations.

MARTY: Thank you, and as your president, I'm committed to…what should I commit to?

JAKE: Why don't you say maintaining safety and reviewing job assignments?

MARTY: I'm committed to safety and job assignments and to show you my integrity I plan to continue my work in research and development until such time as those responsibilities are reassigned. Something is sure to develop.

JAKE: (Clapping) Great speech.

MARTY: Thank you Jake. I felt pretty good about it. I felt confident.

JAKE: Well Mr. President...

MARTY: Come on now. You should still call me Marty! We're still a team.

JAKE: I appreciate that Marty. Just want you to know I'm respectful of your higher position.

MARTY: And I appreciate your appreciation.

JAKE: There's still the unresolved matter of the hole in the bag.

MARTY: Sure. Sure. Go on up and check it out...as a matter of safety.

JAKE: I'm afraid I can't do that, Marty.

MARTY: And why not?

JAKE: I have an executive position. And as an executive I can identify a potential safety issue, but I can't do anything about it. The safety responsibilities of my position have never been required beyond that.

MARTY: I'm feeling a little thawed about that.

JAKE: I can understand that. New position as president, and already you have to resolve a crisis. Need I remind you that you were going to consider re-evaluating the responsibilities of the job positions? You promised the voter, which would be me. You already started. Research and development is now part of the position of being president.

MARTY: You're right about that, Jake. But I was thinking my particular situation was temporary.

JAKE: I'd like to make a suggestion, Mr. President... Marty. I think you need a grunt.

MARTY: A grunt?

JAKE: A working stiff to take care of things like…work. Then you can do the executive work as an executive president ought to have the privilege to do. Making all presidential-like decisions; research, development, accounting, safety. When we counted the frozen peas together that was teamwork, like equals, but things have changed.

MARTY: You're right, Jake, after the decisions, somebody still has to do the work.

JAKE: (Pointing to himself) Honestly, I don't mind. You can rename my executive vice-president position. Change the title, reconfigure the work.

MARTY: Why would you agree to that?

JAKE: Seeing as you're so efficient with your presidential responsibilities and seeing as development is part of those responsibilities, worker frozen pea could be a newly developed position. I figure I should get first crack at the job.

MARTY: Won't you miss the life of an executive?

JAKE: Not at all. I don't get a salary and seems to me maybe I could have some flexible work time. Yeah, I'd kinda like that.

MARTY: Flexible work time?

JAKE: I'd like to start as soon as I'm hired and start with taking a look at that hole.

MARTY: Then you're hired.

JAKE: Thanks Marty.

MARTY: Congratulations.

JAKE: Well, I'm off. I'll climb up to the top of the bag and check for any safety issues that might need resolving.

(Jake climbs up to the top of the bag and looks out.)

JAKE: Marty?

MARTY: Yes Jake.

JAKE: I'm pleased to report that there are no safety issues to be concerned about here. This hole is only big enough for one pea to slip through. So since the peas in the bag are frozen together until the Bergmans get a new refrigerator in maybe another ten years when there might be a chance of slight de-thaw, all is well.

MARTY: Excellent.

JAKE: And Marty?

MARTY: Yes Jake.

JAKE: I regret to inform you that I'm resigning from my position as grunt-frozen pea.

MARTY: You just got the job! We've worked as a team.

JAKE: Not enough for me anymore. This bag has limited opportunities. See ya.

(Jake starts to climb through the hole.)

MARTY: You've climbed up to that hole before? You've looked out of the hole?

JAKE: That I have but on my own time Marty, not during working hours. There's a re-sealable freezer bag over there. I'm getting into it.

MARTY: Why?

JAKE: There's peas and carrots in that bag, and those carrots are gorgeous! I estimate that there are about fifty-eight carrots for every green pea. I just might retire.

MARTY: What about the accounting?

JAKE: Just subtract one, that would be me, from the last total. Then you won't have to count no more. I believe your theory is correct. Frozen green peas last forever.

Nice knowing yous. If I'm gonna be around forever, I'm gonna have a good time.

(Lights Out)

End of Play

My Mother My Wife

"We live in an age when unnecessary things
are our only necessities."

Oscar Wilde

Characters

Christian (Chris) Cortez: Son

Ignacio Cortez: Father, husband

Musician

Setting

Present Day. A two-bedroom apartment in New York
City.

*Author's Note: The characters move back and forth between the two
rooms, sometimes meeting in the center.*

Lights Rise

(Ignacio sits on a chair in one room looking at items in a box.
Christian sits in another room while looking at letters and
documents.)

(Lights Out)

Lights Rise

IGNACIO: (Entering room with Chris, while holding a tie) Chris.

CHRIS: Yeah Dad.

IGNACIO: Look at this.

CHRIS: You have a tie.

IGNACIO: It's yellow.

CHRIS: (Looking) It's a yellow tie.

IGNACIO: Amarillo. What straight man wears a yellow tie?

CHRIS: I guess you do, Dad. Or are you trying to tell me something?

IGNACIO: I don't wear this anymore. It was in your mother's junk box. Everyone else in the world has a junk drawer. Your mother had a junk box.

CHRIS: Dad, you don't have to go through Mom's junk box. Let Aunt Millie…

IGNACIO: Busy body Millie. Bochinchera. Millie is waiting to poke around and get her hands on your mother's things. You didn't ask her to come over, did you?

CHRIS: No Dad. But family shouldn't have to ask. Aunt Millie should look at Mom's …

IGNACIO: She should look at nothing. She wouldn't understand about anything in Melissa's junk box. And I'm boxing all the clothes for the Peace House Women's Shelter.

Millie never liked me. Now, there's more reason for her not to like me.

(Exit Ignacio. He puts on the tie. He picks out a stack of envelopes from the junk box and returns to Chris's room.)

IGNACIO: These were in the box. They have your name on them. (Exits)

(Sounds: Latin rhythms)

CHRIS: These letters are sealed. Funny. Why would Mom address these letters and never send them?

IGNACIO: (Humming and moving to the Latin music alone. Then he dances into Chris's room.) Your old man still has the moves. (Exits)

CHRIS: Maybe it's the magic of the tie.

IGNACIO: That night was magic. I can hear the music. I can see the spotlight.

(Pausing as the music becomes more intense) Your mother wore a silky yellow dress that flowed as she moved. Black fishnet tights and yellow dance panties.

CHRIS: Stop, Dad.

IGNACIO: The finals at the Latin Hideaway were the event everybody in the neighborhood looked forward to. We only got in the finals because of your mother. In the finals, you had to dance every style… merengue, salsa on two, cumbia, bacchante, and I remember a little American…maybe it was the hustle. Your mother was perfect in every way. Suave. The spotlight followed us across the floor. No one could tell she was leading me. (Walking into Chris's room) Ask me if we won.

CHRIS: Did you win Dad?

(Soft musical improvisation)

IGNACIO: (Exiting) No. The spotlight blinded me. Tripped your mother. Her heel broke, and she fell. Your Aunt Millie blamed me. Another red mark on her Ignacio the bum list. Not your mother. She was always forgiving. She was always optimistic. *"Next year, Iggy."* Laughing it off, she said, *"We'll try another color."*

CHRIS: (Looking at a large envelope) Mom kept all of my report cards since kindergarten.

IGNACIO: She was proud of you.

(Music fades)

IGNACIO: (Walking into bedroom) Do you know, I've always been proud of you?

CHRIS: Sure, Dad. Different from Mom. You have another way of showing you're proud. You tell other people. You don't tell me. "My son, the pre-med student with a full scholarship!"

IGNACIO: (Exiting) I'm not a talker. Not that way. (Entering Chris's room) Was that a problem? Did you miss something when you were a kid because I never used words like, "I'm proud of you"?

CHRIS: Naw. Mom was your translator.
> *Your Dad loves you, Chris.*
> *Your Dad is proud of you, Chris.*
> *Your Dad misses you, Chris.*

You did the actions. Mom did the actions and the words.

IGNACIO: I'm sorry.

CHRIS: Nothing to be sorry about. I'm fine…before this…I did well. I had a mother and a father. How lucky is that?

IGNACIO: We did our best. (Exiting) Even when there were problems.

CHRIS: What was that Dad?

IGNACIO: (Picking up photo) There's a photo of your Mom in uniform after her commendation. Do you want it?

CHRIS: You keep it, Dad. We're saving memories, not erasing them.

(Sound: Soft erratic music)

IGNACIO: I didn't recognize her out of uniform. She was off-duty. Came into the bodega for a few things. I was managing the store for your grandfather while he was wintering in DR. Small, neighborhood store. The people who came in were like his family. He didn't accept credit cards. No one had them anyway. He let people run tabs and pay him when their checks came in. Now every store, even a Mom & Pop, has surveillance cameras.

CHRIS: (Reading a letter) *My Dear Son Christian,*

Angels are walking with you, Chris. With every step you take, your success is being planned by your guardian angels. Your photo is in my cap. You're always with me. In my heart, in my mind, in my soul.

Besos y abrazos,

Mom

(Sound: Strong erratic music)
(Spotlight)

IGNACIO: It was like this. She comes to the counter.

What's your name?
Iggy. What's your name, beautiful?
Melissa Fuentes. I'm a cop. Iggy, stay calm.
She shows me her shield.
There's a kid in the refrigerator section with a gun.
You have to shoot him.

Iggy, I need you to lie on the floor and call 911. Tell them there's a potential shooter in the store and an officer in need of assistance. We're going to walk out of here alive if you do what I say. The kid too.

CHRIS: (Reading a letter) My Dear Son Christian,

81

Every action results in a reaction. Some actions can't be undone. You can't reach back and change taking someone's life. You have a good head. Use it. Think first before you act. You don't want a life filled with regret.

Besos y abrazos,

Mom

IGNACIO: I did what she said but all the time, I'm thinking, these female cops get people killed. I couldn't see what happened, but I could hear everything. When he got loud. She lowered her voice. I heard the chime from the front door opening.

(Sound: Sirens)

IGNACIO: She showed her badge out the storefront window.

You did good, Iggy. You're safe. Back-up is outside. Just a scared kid. He'll be picked up.

IGNACIO: I see her gun underneath her jacket. I screamed at her.

You took a big chance with my life, lady.

She screamed at me.

You're alive, right? My job was to make sure everyone was safe. Including keeping that kid safe from himself if I could. He was staring at the frozen pineapple trying to make a decision whether to hold you up. What do you have in your cash register? Less than fifty? Yeah, well I told him you had nothing. I gave him a deuce and told him to never come in your piss-poor store again.

(Spotlight Out)

IGNACIO: I made her a Cubano with lots of pickles.

CHRIS: *(Reading a letter)* *My Dear Son Christian,*
Remember to make the most out of each moment. We don't know how many we have.

Besos y abrazos,

Mom

IGNACIO: (Walking into Chris's room) Here's a list.

CHRIS: For what?

IGNACIO: Of what. Your mother's favorite places for homemade pickles on the lower east side. Those places are disappearing (Walking out of the room). That's why your abuelo moved back to DR. He said the city wasn't the same anymore. And he was too old to change with it.

CHRIS: Are we going to see Mom's old buddies today?

IGNACIO: We'll see all of them. (Digging through the box and taking out handcuffs and showing Chris)

IGNACIO: "Lock me up, Melissa. I surrender."

CHRIS: Not funny, Dad.

IGNACIO: Yeah. Yeah. Your mother never thought so either. This is home. This is the job. Separate. No games. No spill-over. That's why she was such a good cop. She was focused.

CHRIS: We're two people in the same picture, seeing something else. There was spill-over. Just enough to get me straight. After the third strike, I got the message.

IGNACIO: Three strikes? How come I don't know anything about this?

CHRIS: The way Mom wanted it. And the way I wanted it.

IGNACIO: (Walking into bedroom) Why?

CHRIS: Mom thought you would be too soft. And she wanted me to stay the model kid in your eyes. And me? What Dominican kid wants to admit to his father that his mother kicked his ass?

IGNACIO: So?

CHRIS: I'll spare you the details. I was hanging with a bad crew. I wanted to get the nerdy head-in-the-books label off my back. I always did things under the wire only enough for a ticket or a warning. After the third time, Mom served it up cold. I didn't do anything. I didn't do anything. She had some of her buddies pick me up in a patrol car, cuff me, and then put me in a room. No cameras. Everyone ignored what was happening. Then Mom came in and gave me a lesson. The lesson ended with, *"Is this the kind of life you want? Criminal."* After a lockdown for a few hours, a cop comes in and says I can leave. A case of mistaken identity... Those cuffs from her box... probably the ones she used on me.

IGNACIO: (Walking out of room) Secrets. (Looks through the box. Takes out two Christmas Santa's helper's hats. He puts one on.)

CHRIS: Sometimes secrets are necessary.

IGNACIO: (Walks into Chris's room and gives him a hat) A little fun with our sorrow.

(While he watches Chris put on the hat) Who are we?

CHRIS: Dominican Santa's helpers.

IGNACIO: Dominican leprechauns lost at the North Pole. We wore these to the precinct office party every year. (Handing a folded baby blanket to Chris)

CHRIS: This must be...

IGNACIO: At least twenty years old. Your mom made the trim by hand. After her shift, she came home and crocheted the edging. Keep this with your things. For your ninos.

CHRIS: (Taking the blanket) I have to finish the school thing first.

IGNACIO: There's no perfect time. (Picking up a menu) Want to order some sandwiches?

(Reading) Jamon y Queso, Pollo, Pernil, your mother's favorite Cubanao. They all come with papa fritas.

CHRIS: I can't eat until it's over.

IGNACIO: They have sliders.

CHRIS: (Reading a letter) *My Dear Son Christian,*

You'll always be my dear son Christian. I know you'll stay on a good path for yourself with your education and career. I don't worry about that. I want you to be a good husband and a good father one day…if you want. Of course I would love to chase after some little Christian or little Christina after I retire from the police force. Forgiveness is a life skill you'll need no matter what choices you make for yourself. If you can forgive people and move on, that skill will serve you your whole life. I worry that you'll have a problem with forgiveness…with your father. What happened between your father and I is our issue. You're our son…together. Nothing that happened between us changes that. We both love you.

Forgive…the only way to have the big beautiful life you deserve.

Besos y abrazos,

Mom

CHRIS: (Walking toward his father holding the letter) Dad. What's this?

IGNACIO: (Walking towards Chris holding a Baptism dress for a baby) Christ was the ultimate example of forgiveness. Did your mother name you Christian believing the life of Christ would guide you?

CHRIS: What did you do to Mom?

IGNACIO: This was yours. I told your mother you could wear the whole outfit except the bonnet. Baptism is the only time a male can get away with wearing a dress without being questioned.

CHRIS: What did you do to mom?

IGNACIO: You did look cute. Even after you vomited your breakfast over the front…

CHRIS: (Squaring off with his father) Tell me.

IGNACIO: Your mother liked her quiet time after the job. She'd sit in the car and write to you. She didn't want to talk about it. I swore I'd never open them. Your mom called the letters "pequenos momentos tranquilos," small quiet moments. Saved treasure that would become yours one day.

CHRIS: Mom was everything to me.

IGNACIO: I married your mother's job when I married her. I wasn't ready.

CHRIS: Ready for what? Mom was a good cop.

IGNACIO: Our time together became next to nothing when she decided she wanted to move up in rank. I wanted her to get out early. Maybe have another kid. She said, a man wouldn't be asked to make that kind of a decision.

(Pause)

Her name is Josie. We have two kids. They live in Queens.

CHRIS: Who are you talking about?

IGNACIO: My other family.

(Chris and Ignacio pause and look at each other. Then they face forward as the walls of the apartment disappear. The setting is now a memorial service in a hall filled with a crowd of police officers and community members. Chris and Ignacio stand at a podium.)

(Sound: Bars of America the Beautiful)

CHRIS: On behalf of my mother

IGNACIO: On behalf of my wife

CHRIS & IGNACIO: We proudly accept this honorary promotion to Detective First Grade.

CHRIS: Her fellow officers, I know, will remember her as a professional with a calm head and calm but steady hands. Some of you know a little more about my mother's hands than others.

IGNACIO: I'm a musician. In my world, I would say my wife could feel the music before it was heard.

CHRIS: I think about my mom every day. No matter how old you become, if you have a loving mother, you can never get her voice out of your head.

IGNACIO: It was never easy being the spouse of a cop. Melissa told me, fear never makes her decisions and that I should remember the excellent training she received from the NYPD that guided her on every job.

(Pause)

She was shot in cold blood during a quiet moment alone. The coward that shot her removed an innocent wife, sister, and mother from her family. These senseless acts of violence are evil and unjustified.

CHRIS: I want to thank Commanding Officer Jordan for the generous donation he offered from the Widows and Orphans Fund.

IGNACIO: We want to offer those funds back to the department for the Police Athletic League. Melissa felt strongly that young people could be directed to make better choices if they had mentors and positive relationships with caring adults.

(Sounds: Musical Tribute)

CHRIS: I'd like to close this memorial by sharing a letter found in my mother's car the night she was murdered.

My Dear Son Christian,

See all people as you see yourself. Everyone needs love and kindness. Protect yourself from harm and protect all those in your care.

Love, Mom

(Fade to Black)

End of Play

Baby Doll

Shoe Fly

Character

Clara: A woman

Setting

Present Day. New York City. Clara and Antoine's apartment. There is a bed and a night table. Clara is lying down in bed with her legs spread open. She wears intimate apparel underneath a bathrobe. She waits for her husband to arrive.

Lights Rise

CLARA: (She counts aloud) One one-thousand, two one-thousand, three one-thousand, four one-thousand, five one-thousand. Get up sister. This is the day the Lord has made. This is the day the Lord has made for me. (Gets up from bed and paces the floor) Three minutes to walk down the stairs. Ten minutes to the subway, three hours downtown and back, good…good… No…maybe he'll go to neighborhood stores… No subway…twenty minutes, thirty minutes. Then maybe this isn't the day.

(Looking at newspaper sales circulars) All of these stores, which ones will you go to, Antoine? (Showing the circulars) He prefers to be in the store and try them on himself. We went to the store together the first few months. He held each shoe in his hand like he was holding a baby. Every style, every color, every texture fascinated him. I was fascinated too, until I learned that the shopping spree wasn't about fashionable shoes.

Don't go there. (Lifts some clothing to reveal skin) Don't you see any scars?

I understand. My scars are mostly on the inside of me now. (Pulls down clothing and covers skin. Takes a photo album from the night table and opens it.)

You have it going on, don't you, Tamika. All of your boxes checked. Handsome. Educated. Good job. Money in the bank. Family with a good reputation. And a sexless, lifeless marriage. Where is he? Strayed? Married and alone.

I'm a good girl. I'm his Baby Doll. Antoine would never stray from me.

Daddy goes to work and then he comes home to me. He gets what he wants the way he wants it. You don't get it. Men say they want a beautiful, intelligent, and ambitious woman. A match. All a man really wants is a baby doll. An imaginary virgin.

Joshua, your sexting is no replacement for the real thing.

And you, Ethel, sex only for children… Church, kids, kitchen…

How's that working for you? I skipped the line on that one.

I see you married a whole family, Nadia. Not what you expected? You thought you were marrying the man? Hello!

Finding love isn't easy. Good luck with being alone your whole life, Randy.

You put your masks on everyday…just like me…

My grateful book… (Finds book and reads from it)

May 5th 2014

Riding through Central Park. I sat on the handlebars. Riding fast. Wind in my face. My body pressed up against him. Stopping at the vendor for Italian ices. Sitting by the duck pond talking about our dreams.

October 2nd 2016

Marry me, Clara. Let's be happy together. Always sweet. Always tender. I was the one who wanted to spice it up. (She puts on jeans and a tee shirt) A little interesting. Small things. Nibbles, spanks. He liked me on top. Never bondage. That's glorified slavery. I'm not judging. You do you. I do me. A little pain with submission. Suspense. Surprise.

I made it change. Then it kept changing…and changing…out of my control…out of my desire…I was lost. It wasn't me. I knew it was different when I had no power to say no.

Honeymoon Bra (Putting on a brassiere) Cancun. That was the first time he used his shoes on me… A woman is supposed to remember her honeymoon…right? He parted my lips, put blood on them, and kissed me. It was my blood. I called his mother when the ship docked. She asked me, "Does Antoine still like shoes?"

(Holding a brassiere) Birthday Bra. (Sung) "It's his birthday, happy birthday, it's his birthday, happy birthday."

Pushed up against the wall in the bathroom for the real birthday bash. You heard everything. I know, because none of you would look at me when I served you slices of his cake with my bruised, shaking hand.

(Putting on jeans and a Tee shirt) You heard me screaming. Crying. Begging him to stop. Are you okay, sister? Need something, sister? You saw blood on all of my clothes when we were in the laundry room together. Thanks for the stain remover, but it only works on clothes. Kind face, closed lips.

Who worries about me? Who helps break the spell on me? Help me surrender that feeling of wanting love at any cost. Help me surrender my fear of being alone.

What am I asking you for? You can't do that for yourself.

(Folds laundry from a laundry basket and puts it in a suitcase. Holds a brassiere) First year anniversary underwire, push up, with a little extra padding. I had a little trouble that day. I made a mistake. But I'm lucky, my man always gave me a second chance…time to make the necessary correction.

"You left some hair—it looks like a landing strip—You know I want it clean"

I'm sorry Daddy, I get razor bumps when I shave every

"Making excuses Baby Doll. Never make excuses."

Yes Daddy.

"Clean yourself up next time. I want to see all that skin bare clean. I'll let it go this time because I'm an understanding Daddy. Who's the best Daddy?"

You're the best Daddy, Antoine.

"Now suck me good and hold it until I'm ready."

Yes Daddy—anything for you, Daddy.

"Who's the Baby doll?"

(Looking in a hand mirror) I'm the baby doll. I can make my world beautiful by making myself beautiful.

I'm worried about Antoine. His mother strapped his arms to a bedpost and beat him. For every nothing thing... He lost his gloves. Bad grades on his report card. Didn't finish his chores. He needs me. He's never really been loved before. I'm good at this job. I can love him. The way he wants. I can love him. Antoine can't be happy without me.

(Sitting on bed) I'm all clean for you, Daddy—no hair on my

"I told you I want a little hair rubbing on me"

You said

"Are you telling me what I said, Baby Doll?"

No Daddy.

"Go get my work boots—the ones with the steel toes."

No, Daddy— I'll be a good girl— It won't happen again—the hair will grow back—

"Get me my boots, Baby Doll. I have to help you to be a good girl."

Yes, Daddy....

Can I get your loafers? I had the heels fixed for you... new lifts and steel taps.

Daddy, please don't use the boots.

"Sh…stop begging. I'm training you to become a lady. Ladies don't beg. Alright, Baby doll, we can use the loafers.

(Pause)

"That was real nice, Baby doll.
You were respectful—you didn't cry.
Kiss Kiss.
Now lie across the bed and get ready for me.
I'm going to have my smoke outside.
Then I'll be back to finish my business."

Yes, Daddy.

(Pause)

He finished his business. His business almost finished me. He used an ice pick. I thought he only liked shoes.

(Reading from the grateful book) January 26, 2021.* I'm still alive. This is what my squirrel money is for.

(She opens a drawer in the night table. She searches for money in an envelope. She takes out a single dollar bill. She reads a note found in the envelope.) "I see everything you do, baby doll."

(She takes out several boxes of Antoine's shoes and throws them at the wall.)

Timberland, Alexander Mc Queen, Gucci, Ferragamo, Versace, Steve Madden, Cole…

Antoine's new shoes. He's going to break them in… on me.

(She pulls out stiletto-heeled shoes from under the bed.)

New shoes. New shoes.

(She demonstrates how she will use the heels of the shoes when Antoine arrives.)

(Moves a chair by the door and sits on the chair) He went shopping in the neighborhood. Ten minutes down the street. Five minutes for a smoke. Three minutes up the stairs. This is the day the Lord has made. My destiny is in my hand. I'm ready. I wonder how Antoine will like my new shoes? I'm ready.

(Lights Out)

End of Play

Production Note: The audience sits in "stadium style." The play is staged in the center. The audience can see the play and each other. The audience represents the silent observers.

In performance, the present date is used.

Moo Better Blues

More than a Pretty Face

Characters

Daisy: Mature Holstein cow

Derrick Johns: Slaughter Adviser, Slaughter House Unlimited

Curtis: Jamaican born co-owner of Safe Pastures Frozen Yogurt

Aaron: Co-owner of Safe Pastures Frozen Yogurt

Setting

Present Day. Heifer Consultation Room at Slaughter House Unlimited. Mr. Johns sits behind his desk. Enter Daisy.

Lights Rise

DERRICK: Moo.

DAISY: Moo back to you.

DERRICK: I'm sorry…I can't resist. Knock Knock. Please indulge me.

DAISY: Who's there?

DERRICK: Daisy.

DAISY: Daisy who?

DERRICK: Daisy Moo Better.

DAISY: That's not funny.

DERRICK: Yeah it is. You know…you moo like a cow…but you moo better than a regular cow because you moo and you can talk. So you moo better.

DAISY: That's not funny.

DERRICK: A pleasure, no an honor to meet you Daisy. And may I say…that's an outstanding rump you have. Cows your age usually have sagging utters and a wrinkled up rump. You're beautiful and brainy.

DAISY: I don't know whether to say "thank you" or cringe. We know I'm not here because I have a beautiful body.

DERRICK: Daisy, please sit, stand…whichever you prefer. I had a collapsible stall built for you to use during our consultation. You're welcome to try it and see if it will help you feel more comfortable. Shall I get it?

DAISY: I was **born** in a stall. I spent my adult life in a pasture.

DERRICK: Oh…let me review my notes… Yes. Grass fed, no steroids, no hormones; upstate family farm… got it. Sorry.

DAISY: I'll accept your apology, I suppose…

DERRICK: I'm so fascinated with you Daisy. If only clean living could explain your intelligence, this would be a simple slaughter advisement meeting. Heck… you're the reason I have this job. If it weren't for you I'd still be on the minimum wage butcher line in the factory cutting up steaks.

DAISY: Is this the part of the slaughter consultation when I say, you're welcome?

DERRICK: Daisy…family owned and nurtured cows are nothing new. But the discovery of your remarkable intelligence has completely revolutionized the cow slaughter industry. I mean, Daisy…there wouldn't be slaughter advisers if it weren't for you, and I the first slaughter adviser in the industry.

DAISY: How nice for you! For me…this consultation is just about my life and death story.

DERRICK: Quite frankly, if we don't discover some more intelligent cows soon, I'm out of this job as fast as I got it.

DAISY: Back to the blood and guts line then?

DERRICK: I understand your focus is on your personal issues, but keep in mind that Slaughter Unlimited and the whole notion of advising a heifer before death is only taking place because of you. The discovery through you that cows could have intelligence comparable to humans has forced us to consider kill-procedures that are more cow friendly. Again…thanks for getting me off that factory line.

DAISY: Just out of curiosity Mr. Johns, what kind of training did they give you to do this job?

DERRICK: The company is still working it out. This is a new industry, and there aren't rules and regulations mandated by the state yet.

DAISY: Lucky me.

DERRICK: You're a hoot. Or should I say hooters! Don't be concerned. I had a community college introduction to social work course. I also attended a special seminar on Death and Dying. The affordable health care insurance agent for our company provides it for free for our company. The seminar was actually about understanding the stages of grief for caregivers of people dying from chronic disease, but I'm sure there's something that applies here. You know…like "Mad Cow Disease." And I hope you don't mind, but my boss wants me to take notes from your feedback. We want to continue improving our slaughter advisement procedures.

DAISY: Would you take that taxidermy steer head off the wall while I'm here? I'm offended. It looks like my Dad.

DERRICK: Of course. And I'm making a note: "No animal heads in the consultation room." What if we had more of an Indian theme…you know…like masks for rain dances…and good harvests.

DAISY: Now you're mocking Native Americans. Who else are you going to offend today before I leave?

DERRICK: Just a little fun, Daisy. Everyone knows Indians don't believe in rituals anymore, they run casinos. Besides, I don't have any information about religious affiliations in your case file.

DAISY: I'm not religious, but I'm respectful of human spiritual experiences.

DERRICK: You're amazing.

DAISY: I read on a variety of topics, mostly philosophy, since I'm in this predicament.

DERRICK: How do you manage reading books…I mean hold the book and turn the pages?

DAISY: Farmer Jake ordered audio books for me, and he purchased some noise reduction earphones.

DERRICK: It's not necessary, but I would appreciate if you could tell me your personal cow story. It's not in the case notes…you know…how you found out you were an intelligent cow.

DAISY: Why are you so curious?

DERRICK: Because, you're the only intelligent cow we know about. Because…we don't know how to test for cow intelligence. Because there're thousands of cows that grew up with your clean, country life…so none of this makes sense. Most cows are dumb as dirt.

DAISY: Those are my kin you're calling dumb.

DERRICK: I'm sorry Daisy. I don't think anyone has had to consider political correctness when it comes to cows. Let's be truthful here…you must realize you're a freak of nature…a fantastic freak…but still a freak. I'm just hoping we find more intelligent cows so I can keep my job.

DAISY: I'm just being myself, and I never considered that I was different. The farm was pleasant. Farmer Jake and his family…a few farm hands…all the milking was personal. Farmer Jake played classical music for us while we were milked. I had my own milk bucket with hand painted daisies. Farmer Jake had a beautiful stroke. My udders were never stretched out and sore. Milking was never painful. It was a relief… and almost orgasmic. Relaxing times in the barn. Beautiful days in the pasture. Honestly, I had nothing to talk about. It was a Zen kind of life. I was in a state of bliss every day. Mooo……Mooooo…. Moooooooooooooooooo

DERRICK: Need some tissues?

DAISY: Do you have a towel? Everything changed overnight. I knew Farmer Jake had over-mortgaged the farm. I heard him telling the Mrs. I knew a little about finances and capital improvement. When it comes down to it…wealth and security is all about pluses and minuses. I didn't interfere and offer my opinion. It was their business to work out. The next day a bank officer from Blue State Savings and Loan came by to inspect the herd. He told Farmer Jake that the days of the family farm were over… He told Farmer Jake that the days of the family farm were coming to an end and his only hope of keeping his farm was to become a commercial dairy.

DERRICK: Calm down! You're dropping dung all over the place! Do you know how to use a bathroom?

DAISY: I can't help it… I'm too upset. One by one they came in dressed in white lab coats and white hats. They looked like Klu Klux Klan people for cows. They took the heifers one at a time. Sometimes gangs of four and five men holding down one cow forcing these big plastic tubes with suction grips on her utters, clamping down on the most personal part of a female cow's body. There wasn't tenderness or even care and concern, only assault. I heard my sister cows moo out in shock and pain. They cried out for Farmer Jake. He was obviously outnumbered and powerless to save us. Then I heard one say, "Let's get that big heifer." I knew he was talking about me. I was the largest cow in the herd… I tried to remain calm…there was no escape…then when one of the gang touched my utter…let's just say I expressed how I felt.

DERRICK: You mean you talked?

DAISY: "The Art of War" by Sun Tzu, chapter one… laying plans…assessing outcomes. I determined that waging war would be futile with an army of one. So I decided to appeal to their higher selves, the compassionate nature of humanity.

DERRICK: Then you talked?

DAISY: I spoke without fear, drawing on the teachings of Martin Luther King Jr. and Gandhi. But they were really my words. I had something I wanted to talk about for the first time, and I took the opportunity to say anything and everything I wanted to say about my condition, and the mistreatment of my sisters. I looked around hoping the rest of the herd would rally with me and verbally refuse to be milked by machines, but none of the other cows supported me. Everyone was silent. I was angry. No social movements exist without solidarity of the masses. But I was alone.

DERRICK: Maybe they were typically stupid cows.

DAISY: Moooooooooooo or maybe they were scared victims of oppression who didn't have the courage to resist.

DERRICK: Wow…some story… After you're dead, an autopsy of your brain might give us some indications of why you're intelligent, but in the meantime…we're clueless. All the cows from your herd are dumb as dirt.

DAISY: This slaughter counseling is supposed to be a comfort to me, not an opportunity for you to satisfy your curiosity and give you personal time to interact with the freak!

DERRICK: I was over the line, Daisy, by asking you about personal matters, but I can see you have a misconception about what we're doing here. This is slaughter advisement, not slaughter counseling. This meeting is not touchy-feely to help you feel comfortable with the killing process; it's to provide you with a choice over your death.

DAISY: Mooooooooooooooooo

DERRICK: And don't get upset and drop your dung. This office already stinks. You have the intelligence to choose your method of death and Slaughter Unlimited is committed to giving you that choice. Keep in mind, Daisy, that this is a new industry and we're providing this service as a courtesy. We're under no obligation by law to provide you with any special consideration.

DAISY: Moooooooooo

DERRICK: You're a cow. We own you. You existed a little longer than those dumb heifers in your Holstein herd because we chose to keep you around... for amusement.

DAISY: I need an attorney. Maybe I could have a case argued before the Supreme Court?

DERRICK: Sorry, Daisy. The Supreme Court isn't ready to hear a cow about a cow. They're backlogged with cases about humans.

DAISY: What about Jay Leno? If I could get on his show, I know…

DERRICK: His show is cancelled.

DAISY: What about the Vatican?

DERRICK: Yes, I have a note from the Vatican. (Opens letter) I'll read it to you. It says, "It's a miracle." Did you actually think the Vatican was going to consider you for sainthood? You're not Roman Catholic!

DAISY: I'm not saying another word until you get Farmer Jake.

DERRICK: Slaughter Unlimited owns your black and white rump. So shut up and cooperate.

DAISY: (Kicking the office door) Help me…Mooooooooo… Help me…Mooooooooooooo…Let me out of here.

DERRICK: (Throwing objects) Shut up or I'll get the collapsible stall and lock you in it until I'm finished with processing your paperwork.

DAISY: (Sobbing) I need Farmer Jake. Let me talk to him, please. He loves me. He'd never want me to be treated this way. I was supposed to spend the rest of my life in the pasture with my own country mini barn. I was going to listen to classical music, practice yoga, and Pilates every day. That's the kind of life Farmer Jake wanted for me.

DERRICK: This is so cool! I've never seen a heifer beg for her life. Farmer Jake can't help you now, Daisy. The bank foreclosed on the farm. All the Holstein cows, a few steers, and some new born calves, or fresh veal meat, as I like to call them, have already gone up the conveyor belt. You're here as a result of a special agreement Farmer Jake made with the bank to give you consideration because you're able to reflect on your death. You're worth more to us dead than alive. Everybody wants a piece of you, Daisy. There's a bidding war going on for your feet with every nation in the Caribbean. Something about some magical peas and rice... Are we clear now, Daisy?

DAISY: Slaughter is slaughter, no matter how you spin it.

DERRICK: My turn to share now, Daisy. I like my job because I make more money than a minimum-wage line butcher. That's it. I grew up around farms. Friday nights we played shoot the cow, bb guns…great fun. But my favorite Friday night game was "Tip the Cow." Two ways to play. Ride in the pick-up trucks as fast as you can until the cow runs into a barn or tree and knocks herself out, or, on the count of three, we stand on the ground and push as hard as possible until the heifer falls over. But there were everyday pleasures like poking cows with pitchforks. I remember leaving bloody cows' heads for pranks. Not a big deal. So you see, Daisy, I know from personal experience that cows, as I said before, are "dumb as dirt." Excuse me, I should have said, "Dumber than dirt." You're a freak, and it makes no difference to me that you can think, and study, and rattle off some philosophy crap and, hell, twist your body into yoga positions…you're still meat!

DAISY: You're right. I'm a freak and a nice piece of rump for a tailgate party, racks of ribs for a barbecue, and cow pieces for West Indian peas and rice. I wish I couldn't feel, understand, reflect, and consider my life. It's only because I can that my pain is more than physical. My soul cries out for mercy. (She sings her rendition of the BB King classic, "The Trill is Gone")

The trill is gone
The thrill is gone away
The thrill is gone Mr. Johns
The trill is gone away.
You know you done me wrong DERRICK
And you'll be sorry someday.*

DERRICK: (While clapping sarcastically) Moo moo moo too bad. I want to finish this up. It's almost lunch time. By the way…nice lunch suggestions. I think I'll get some barbecue beef ribs with Devil May Care hot sauce at Rudy's Rib Shack or maybe I'll have cow foot with peas and rice at the Steak & Take Café. So many choices, and only one hour for lunch. I'll get take-out for later. I really love the way Koreans make ribs…. yum…and a new restaurant opened in the neighborhood. Looking at you inspires me to overeat. (Sound Effect: Papers rustling) Let's go through the choices and then you'll give you hoof print stamp of acceptance. Just proof that you've been advised and with free will you chose your slaughter plan.

DAISY: I want to live.

DERRICK: (Laughs hysterically) No more time for jokes. Living…not an option. Religious or secular?

DAISY: Moo.

DERRICK: People language please. Do you want to get blessed by a Rabbi or stunned and slit at the neck by an Arab?

DAISY: Moo.

DERRICK: You can't choose both. You can be kosher meat or Halal.

DAISY: Moo.

DERRICK: Okay…I'll accept your non-answers to mean you want secular. (Sound Effect: Papers rustling) Texas style or traditional?

DAISY: Would you explain Texas style, please?

DERRICK: Sure…a small band of cowboys will lynch you up to a tree with rope, whip you until they break the skin on your hide, decapitate you, and I get your head for my wall.

DAISY: Is there something else?

DERRICK: You don't seem to be the kinky sort, so I wasn't going to mention it. There's S&M. We let some degenerates' gang rape you then we turn you over to a mob of butchers dressed in black leather that take turns assaulting you with cleavers. The assaults continue until your last moo.

DAISY: Have you any compassion?

DERRICK: No. (Rustling papers) I'll need your hoof print here verifying that you rejected all presented alternatives. That means you'll join what's left of the herd guided up the conveyor belt.

CURTIS & AARON: Daisy. Where are you? Daisy. Daisy.

DAISY: I hear voices calling me.

DERRICK: No, you don't. Put your hoof print here.

DAISY: Moo?

CURTIS & AARON: (Opening and slamming doors) Moooooooooo Daisy. Where are you?

DAISY: (Moving around the office) Moo. Mooooooooooooooooooooooooo. Moo. Moo. Mooooooooooooooooooooo. People are here for me. Open the door.

DERRICK: Nobody is here for you. I need your hoof print.

DAISY: (Kicks the door) Open the door, Johns.

CURTIS & AARON: Are you in dere, Daisy?

DAISY: Moo!

DERRICK: No one is getting in here before you put your hoof print on those papers.

DAISY: Open the door, Mr. Johns unless you want to feel the power of an angry eight hundred pound heifer all over you.

(Sound Effect: Door opening)

CURTIS: Dis place is blessed. Dere's dung everywhere. Daisy…we be lookin everywhere for you gal.

AARON: Everywhere.

DERRICK: Get out. This is a private office. How did you get past security?

CURTIS: A little magic, Mon.

AARON: Yeah, a little magic.

CURTIS: We need you to let de cow go free, Mon.

AARON: Yeah…let de cow go free.

DERRICK: Who are you people?

CURTIS: I'm Curtis. And me Mon here is Aaron.

AARON: Yeah. I'm Aaron.

CURTIS: We have a petition here from COW Amnesty International. All dese people sign papers sayin let de cow go free.

DAISY: Moooooooooooooooooooooooooo

CURTIS: Dat's right, sister. Soon you be free to live, and live righteous.

ARRON: Live righteous.

DERRICK: Slaughter Unlimited owns this cow. She's not going anywhere except up the conveyor belt so we can cut her up for high price meat. She's worth millions.

CURTIS: You should feel of shamed yourself.

ARRON: Yeah, you should feel ashamed.

CURTIS: Tell me sometin, Son. How much of dem millions ya get ta keep for youself?

AARON: Yeah, how much you get?

DERRICK: The money will belong to the company. But I'll get one half of one half percent commission.

CURTIS: And that's the point, son. Dat why we need ya to turn a blind eye. Make yourself useful, Aaron Mon, and pick up de dung we can take back wit us.

AARON: Yeah…pick up de dung…

CURTIS: Turn a blind eye…just let de cow go free. We taking ya to Mooghanistan, a little territory between India and Pakistan where you can live in peace for the rest of your days.

DAISY: Isn't there a war over there?

CURTIS: People fighting people, Daisy…not cows. Cows are sacred, never killed, never eaten. Everywhere you walk people will admire you and praise you…you'll be happy.

DAISY: Mooo Moooo Moooooooooooooo

DERRICK: That heifer's not leaving this office.

CURTIS: Would be a good ting if you would do this without persuasion, but I see we will have to use some magic. Aaron, we need the magic now.

DERRICK: You people are nuts. I don't believe in magic.

CURTIS: It's cash, Mon. All yours free and clear. All you need to do is let our gal Daisy come with us. We already used magic for security. The way is clear. We got a ship waiting for her safe passage.

DERRICK: Are you people drug dealers?

AARON: Drug dealers?

CURTIS: No Mon, we de owners of Curtis 'n Aaron Safe Pastures Frozen Yogurt.

DERRICK: You can make this kind of money selling frozen yogurt?

CURTIS: Lots more.

AARON: Lots more.

CURTIS: It's fat free 'n sugar free. Don't hesitate. You should do dis, Mon.

DERRICK: Okay…but you have to make it seem like I couldn't stop her and she escaped.

DAISY: I can take care of that. (Pushing Derrick's body aggressively against the office wall)

And that was for my father.

CURTIS: Time to leave, Sister.

AARON: I made you some organic vegan weed burgers for the voyage.

DAISY: I don't know how to thank you enough.

CURTIS: You exist. Dat is tanks enuf, Sister.

DAISY: I want to take my Dad with me.

AARON: I haven't picked up all de dung!

DAISY: Don't worry. I can poop more. It's the least I can do.

(Lights Out)

End of Play

Note: *"The Thrill is Gone," Written by Roy Hawkins and Rick Darnell (1951). BB King rendition released (1969).*

Samo Isn't Dead

Cause Dead Ain't Dead

Characters

Caretaker: Mature Black man with "cluttered" speech pattern and an animated communication style (whole body)

JM: Caretaker transformed by Jean-Michel Basquiat's spirit

Gisele: Twenty-something woman

Setting

Circa October 1988. Green-Wood Cemetery. Brooklyn, New York City. The gravesite of Jean-Michel Basquiat.

(In the darkness)

CARETAKER & GISELE: In the beginning, there was the word
And the word was SAMO
Not SAMBO
Not SAM——O
SAME   OH
Same Old Shit

Lights Rise

(Sound: Ravel's Boléro)

(The caretaker alternatively takes sips from a flask, while raking leaves and drawing/writing on the headstones. He is humming a rock/hip hop version of Ravel's Boléro.)

CARETAKER: Medication walks on the boardwalk without shoes.

Want to go to the beach? (Sips from the flask) I'll share my medication.

(Enter Gisele, looking around the cemetery.)

CARETAKER: You're looking for him (Points in the direction of Jean Michel's headstone) Wait. Listen to…

GISELE: I don't hear anything.

CARETAKER: (He hums Boléro with physical animation) Jean Michel loved Ravel.

GISELE: How do you know I'm looking for Basquiat?

CARETAKER: Everyone's looking for Basquiat. You missed the crowds.

GISELE: I don't see the headstone.

CARETAKER: Over there…next to Picasso.

GISELE: Picasso?

CARETAKER: Wait. No. Picasso is buried in Bed Stuy. Look next to Daniel and Charlotte Johnson. Nice couple. They went together…fell off a glacier in the French Alps. Nothing but bone fragments and dust when they were found. Their kids insisted on bringing back every

GISELE: Stop. Can you show me, please?

CARETAKER: May they rest in peace. (Walking to the headstone with Gisele) I thought you'd want to know he was buried next to a loving couple that had loving children. Love is important in life and in

GISELE: (Looking at the headstones covered with graffiti) What happened here?

CARETAKER: (Walking away) I'll leave you to your visit.

GISELE: Are you the caretaker?

CARETAKER: (Looking through the pockets of his work clothes) I have an official badge somewhere.

GISELE: Who marked up these headstones with all of this graffiti?

CARETAKER: (Hiding markers and brushes in his work clothes) Maybe Jean Michel likes it. The Johnson kids do, they're art lovers. I believe their parents, the people I told you about, Daniel and Charlotte, took those kids everywhere to see art… The Brooklyn Museum, The Metropolitan Museum of Art… I think little Danny…, not so little now, took classes…

GISELE: Stop.

CARETAKER: I have to get to my caretaking duties. Over there…here…over there… That's what I do… caretaking…

GISELE: No respect for you mi amour…even in death…

CARETAKER: Art is necessary. Beauty can be ugly. Ugly can be beauty.

GISELE: What did you say?

CARETAKER: You'll have to leave the graveside by five. I have to lock up. You can't stay longer. It won't matter that you're not finished. Have much to talk with Jean about?

GISELE: May I have some privacy, please?

CARETAKER: I'll be over here, over there, taking care of my caretaking care taking. Already raked the leaves in that section. I rake by sections, and then I blur the open spaces with small found objects. I like to play with positive and negative spaces in the landscape.

GISELE: Who are you?

CARETAKER: Only a nobody, somebody who takes care. Call me if you need

GISELE: I won't need anything but privacy. You should know that people need privacy so they can mourn their dead.

CARETAKER: Not too much mourning happens around Jean Michel...confessions and regret...Which are you?

(Exit Caretaker to the opposite side of the graveyard. Gisele in front of the headstone, she takes a simple canvas from her bag and a collection of paints and brushes. She paints throughout her time at the graveside.)

GISELE: Life without permission...working on that... life without regret...that'll have to be for my next life.

∞

JM

Straight lines and polka dots
Why put a polka on a dot on a dot and a dot
and a dot and a dot?
Exclamation point!

∞

GISELE: Maybe you'd like all this graffiti all over your headstone. You could never be like anyone else not in life, not in death.

∞

JM

Muhammed Ali
The greatest

∞

GISELE: I had to wait. I needed time to get here. You understand, right?

∞

JM

Every kid gets a black and white composition
notebook
And then they take it away
"You can keep the book, but remember you
don't own the pages."
Write what you're told.
SAMO

∞

GISELE: When we were in high school, I never liked too many people around me. That hasn't changed.

∞

JM

I'm a prisoner in love with a prisoner in love
with a prisoner in love
Capture me and let me go
Open the door
Ha Ha

∞

GISELE: I would have hung out with you and Al paint-ing your what-so-ever way where ever, but remember me, "Giselle, frightened cat." I thought I was scared of people. I've come a long way since we were seven-teen. Now I know I was afraid of myself.

∞

JM

Cracks in the gas line
Cracks in the pavement

> Cracks in the tile
> Crack the crackers
>
> ∞

GISELE: Do you remember Mr. Longo's math class eight period? You were always cutting class and escaping somewhere to draw…asking me for notes…

> ∞

> JM

> She knows where the gorilla lives five times a day
>
> ∞

GISELE: Cutting to dropping out…I knew that time would come. When you dropped out of school, you dropped out of me and my life…not my heart. All the girls stuck to you. Why couldn't you choose me? Was I too hard, too straight? Did I remind you of your father?

> ∞

> JM

> Brick
> Block
> Blake
> Blue
> Bliss
> Make my list
>
> ∞

GISELE: (Holding up canvas to face the headstone) I've been working on this piece. My hand stopped moving. No energy flowing. Like my hand was frozen every time I picked up the brush.

∞

JM

Wood, fiber, paper, snap
Wood, fiber, paper, snap
Wood, fiber, paper, snap
Jump back

∞

GISELE: You had your own hand. Unmistakably yours. Recognizable as only yours.

∞

JM

Stagecoach
Wells Fargo
Listen
Corporate monsters ruining the ruins

∞

GISELE: I wish I could have been naked. Like you. You validated your own self…your own art. Gisele follows all of the rules. Gisele does what she's told. Gisele lets other people think for her. Gisele the stuck-up girl who can't get stuck to Jean Michel, the beautiful boy every girl wants to be stuck to.

∞

JM

I'll find the missing word
I'll let the missing word go
The words come through me
I don't own them…or do I?

∞

GISELE: I read about you when you were in LA. I had a big plan. Fly to California. Meet Jean Michel at his gallery opening. Surprise you. You knew I loved you. We were friends. Was there a way we could still become lovers? Just thoughts in my dread state. Nothing happened. Nothing could have happened. All the women around you stick to you, licking you like a sugar cube. I wondered if they'd be around for the long... Well, we both know now how that turned out.

∞

JM

Actors don't get shot, "in the real"

Cross out

∞

GISELE: I heard you were looking for the old crowd, the SAMO crowd when...your tumble started. I wasn't around...on purpose...forgive me.

∞

JM

25 cent bag of potato chips

25 cent bag of cheese doodles

Make my tongue orange and large

Measure the size of Negro lips

∞

GISELE: I heard you were looking for the "for real" people. The before people. Those of us who loved you before you were famous to the world and had groupies, and money stuffed in mattresses, and shots lined up along your studio floor, and special tables at restaurants where you used to sift through dumpsters for food. Apartment to apartment. Sofa couch. The Befores.

∞

JM

New Downtown. Lower East.
New Orleans
New Harlem
Enslavement Quarters

∞

GISELE: I know there were a few, like Andy, who embraced you.

∞

JM

Don and Hill explained the debate to me

∞

GISELE: I should have embraced you then...before the tumble...before the spiral...

When you reached out...I should have reached back. Only the Befores, like me, who knew your soul like DNA spilled out on the streets...only the Befores, like me...could have held your hand and led you back by following you.

∞

JM

Humans can be sold
Nuevo style auction blocks and office cubicles

∞

GISELE: I'm sorry.

∞

JM

Now is the time
Go and come back
How will I come back?

A freeeeeeeee man
I'll try Gisele.

∞

GISELE: I know you tried. Couldn't do it by yourself. Your beautiful soul wasn't safe too long in this world.

∞

JM

My life in one bag
Call me the bagman
No, call me the drifter
My body and my mind drift in a mellifluous cloud
I'll find the sweetness of my mother
Drifting

∞

GISELE: My mother always liked you. She never minded you sleeping in the living room. She kept asking me about your mother. You talked about her like she was out of town. Then I found out the truth from Al. People get sick. It's nothing to be ashamed of…

∞

JM

Hard head
Hard mouth
Cast away

∞

GISELE: Hard head.

∞

JM

Hard head
Hard mouth
Cast away

∞

GISELE: You really could draw well. I was a little jealous. I had to work hard at drawing. Graphic art gave me a formula, like math. I could do it without feeling. Follow the formula.

∞

JM

Be careful with my spelling or not

∞

GISELE: There was once when we were thinking one thought…art school…what a dream…we go to Pratt Institute. Your father would have liked that. Official art. Son of immigrants following the rules for success and acceptance.

∞

JM

Had it rough
Made rough and ready

∞

GISELE: That was our fork in the road. I wanted the straight and expected path. Too bad we couldn't stay high school kids forever.

∞

JM

A school dance with other school
Would be, could be, should be, would have
been cool

∞

GISELE: When you drew pictures of flowers and wrote poems on my mother's kitchen curtains, that was when my father put his foot down that you had to find someone else's sofa to live on. I wanted you to

125

know, it wasn't my Mom. She loved how you painted the curtains. Kept them up a long time. My father couldn't stand seeing them. He eventually threw them in the garbage and bought my mother curtains made with a flower print material. Dad passed away before you were rich and famous. I'm sure he would have had a heart attack sooner if he knew he put your original drawings in the trash!

∞

JM

Wino face up
Face down
On the grass
Still warm outside

∞

GISELE: My Dad didn't understand. He didn't feel he had to. He had his own kids and his own problems to worry about. He drowned what worries were possible in his rum punch every night. My mother asked about you often. She told me you were too sweet and open for the world. I didn't understand it then but I understand it now.

∞

JM

The history of the world in one onion
Layer, after layer, after layer, after layer

∞

GISELE: Growing up is like adding layers.

∞

JM

Kayo

∞

GISELE: You had the most beautiful eyes. Intense. You could see straight through me, couldn't you?

∞

JM

Sledgehammer eyes
Take a moment
Sledgehammer eyes

∞

GISELE: You told me you would paint my hazel eyes. Did you ever do that? I wonder if you have undiscovered paintings in boxes somewhere?

CARETAKER: The bus comes today.

GISELE: When we parted ways, I wondered how you would remember me. If you would remember me…

∞

JM

Time for bed
Story time
TV time
Cross out

∞

GISELE: I dreamt about you every night for a while. Mostly they were dreams about you being safe or not. Once I had a dream that you were riding on Godzilla's back like Godzilla was a horse and that you had saddlebags filled with bags of Cheetos and bottles of Pepsi. When I woke up, I thought, perhaps that means Jean Michel is getting plenty to eat of what he wants to eat.

∞

JM

All the shoes on the train
Talking shoes
Different people
Take the shoes walking

∞

GISELE: I've never seen any words or images that suggest me in any of the "Untitled Work."

∞

JM

Crescent Place
Half past eight o'clock

∞

GISELE: That night we walked across the Brooklyn Bridge was special. I used to go there and think of you sometimes. Now, I can come here.

∞

JM

2 PM
3 PM
6 PM
9 o'clock
Red lines in charge

∞

GISELE: Better than going to a museum or gallery. I'd feel out of place. And I don't like other people's thoughts about you getting mixed up with mine. I want mine to stay pure. The Jean Michel I knew.

∞

JM

Flash cards stealing the mind

Freedom fighter in the composition book
Grade = F
Cross out
Grade = A

∞

GISELE: I'll be finished with this. Finished is when I stop. What it is, is what it will be…

CARETAKER: It's almost five o'clock Miss. I'm locking up at five o'clock.

∞

JM

Cross out
Cross out
Add
Take away
Add
Take
Tiny tiny bug crawling on the paper

∞

GISELE: Next to you, here in a cemetery…painting… The Gisele you knew couldn't have done this.

CARETAKER: (Screaming) A las cinco.

∞

JM

The big white whitebread with the center ate out
Pretending to be a doughnut with the crust

∞

GISELE: Leave me alone.

∞

JM

One hundred

One thousand
One billion
Words a week
Walls torn down
One word
∞

GISELE: One simple word can change an entire perspective.

CARETAKER: (Screaming) On ferme à cinq heures.
∞

JM

New education
They want to take away hand-writing
Soon they'll take away hands
∞

GISELE: One line of paint, thick or thin, can change an entire point of view.

CARETAKER: (Screaming) You're gonna have to get out.
∞

JM

Gray
My anatomy book
My Mom
My art band
∞

GISELE: Colors, carefully chosen or not.

CARETAKER: (Screaming) Map fèmen pòt la cinque.
∞

JM

Apartment to apartment

Life on the floors
Cross out
Sofa
Cross out
couch
∞

GISELE: Change the world one painting at a time.
∞

JM

Pillar of salt
Pinch of salt
Salt to taste
Salty saltiness
∞

GISELE: (BeBop scating of "Salt Peanuts") You used everything around you, music, art, dance…
∞

JM

Antidote for love
Je t'aime Mom
∞

GISELE: I go safe. You go as you go. You know as you
know.

CARETAKER: You're lucky the Johnson kids aren't
coming today. They come down during the week after work and they like their privacy too. Just so you
know…they give me a few extra dollars to make sure
the grounds around their parents are nice and neat.
∞

JM

Push and Pull 129

∞

GISELE: It seemed like your inner self was always talking to someone. Someone's conversation coming through your mind and then you answer with new ideas and new words. You let the world in on the conversation.

CARETAKER: I don't ask for the extra money. They're nice people. They know I do a lot of work around here. I hope you're not messing up the grounds over there. Or eating. Or drinking.

∞

JM

Push and Pull class program
Boxes and margins

∞

GISELE: Change people one at a time with a painting.

CARETAKER: I could let you stay a little bitty time after five. Just an itsy bitsy little time. (Singing) The itsy bitsy spider went up the waterspout. Down came the wine and washed the spider out. A few extra dollars would go a long, long way, long, hold up (Sips from flask) long, long way before payday. I need enough to buy a burger and a beverage. (Pause) I'll share. (Singing) How dry I am? How dry I am? Me, myself, and I know how dry I am.

∞

JM

A desired sexual
Sex
You
All

∞

GISELE: You had so little, but you had everything. You weren't a mental slave. (Turning canvas toward headstone) Do you like how it's coming? My hand is freer. The composition is less restricted. I'm exploring bright colors. I can feel the textures lifting off the canvas. This is orgasmic.

∞

JM

Crescent sun
Crescent moon
Redundancy is my friend

∞

GISELE: Perhaps, I should completely start over and make tee shirts and postcards with my art like you did. Maybe there's an Andy Warhol in my life whose glance at my work will propel me into global popularity.

∞

JM

I wrote down her number
Gisele
718-555-4793

∞

GISELE: Feeling so inspired while I sit with you. Nothing graphic artist about this painting. Yes, that's what I do now. I did the straight and narrow all the way. Pratt Institute, then a graphic design job. Nine to five, plan, repeat. I don't believe in poverty. My job pays my rent, buys the food, and will support my baby. I know. Surprise to me too.

∞

JM

Front and back covers are not the front and the
back

∞

GISELE: One of those things. Giselle, straight and narrow, one time I imitate being free. and I get pregnant.
It's a girl, still early (touching belly) not showing much.
Michele Jacqueline, that's what I'm calling her. I'm
already planning her life. Free thinking, uninhibited,
risk-taking in a good way. Like you in your Before
days. She'll have what your before friends had and
still have for you…love. The love for my Michele Jacqueline will surround her and keep her safe. Maybe.

∞

JM

It took four generations
Of four generations
Of four generations
Four generations
And still no access
Gatekeepers everywhere

∞

GISELE: I wish I could have kept you safe…from them.
All the gatekeepers who let you through to the big
money and the big things. You deserved it all. What
did they call you? Radiant Child? (One hand on her belly,
one hand on the headstone) Radiant child, protect my radiant child. I believe the spirits protect us.

∞

JM

The people on the sidewalk shake from the subway

∞

GISELE: Do you remember my brother Philipe?

∞

JM

Dear Dad,
In one thousand years will you love me then?
Sincerely,
Your fake son,
Jean Michel Basquiat

∞

GISELE: He admired everything about you. I was rushing out to class and he asked me for five dollars so he could buy some good pencils and a sketchpad from Pearl Paint on Canal Street. "I want to make graffiti like Jean Michel but not on the street because I don't want to get chased down by the cops.

∞

JM

All this suffering about his finger

∞

GISELE: He wanted to dress like you too, big ugly overcoat and stained up pants. He found some clothing in the trash and put them on one day like he was putting on the costume of his favorite super hero.

∞

JM

Qua qua

∞

GISELE: There was no way my mother was letting him out of the house looking like a bum. My parents didn't want any reminders of the poverty they left before arriving in the states.

∞

JM

Say it fast
Baby say, Baby say, Baby say, Baby say, Baby say, Baby say, Baby say, Baby say, Baby say, Baby say, Baby say, Baby say, Wah Wah

∞

GISELE: He was a beautiful innocent…like you. Focused. One day he said, "I'll make three hundred sixty-five drawings starting from today, the day you left our apartment, one for each day of the year. Jean Michel will be famous. I'll be famous too. The police found him on Willoughby Street, face up with glass all around him. His sneakers were gone. The backpack was gone. The sketchpad and the pencils were on the street next to him.

∞

JM

Empty part with something there
Can't see it
Feel between the lines

∞

GISELE: What is the cost of fame, my friend? Hand-to-mouth living and walking-around change until someone gives your art validation.

∞

JM

Like a Miles Davis tune
Feel between the notes
Nuf said

∞

CARETAKER & GISELE: (Scat, sing, hum, improvisation)

GISELE: What's the cost of being Black? Move through life according to how you feel? Isn't that a luxury for Black people?

∞

JM

Hatch tag your hatch tag

∞

GISELE: I know you would have come to his funeral if you knew.

∞

JM

I'll come by sometime Gisele

∞

GISELE: Everyone wants to live with some lies, right? Feel good lies, escape lies. Lies can console and keep you from crying in the dark. The problem is when self lies catch up with you. Like "IT." The "IT" in the hide and go seek game. IT tags you. Then, what do you do if you don't want to play anymore? But you don't want to get bullied off the playground.

∞

JM

Clean anyone?
Rhetorical

No one is clean

∞

GISELE: No one is perfect.

∞

JM

(Snorting drugs from a paper bag) This is the last
last time I'm doing this. Just a little. Take the
edge off. Back to work. Paint on paint on paint.
Bigger canvas. Mama' the museum. The lights.
The colors. I wanted to paint with my hands
(looking at hands), my naked hands. Help me pick
up the brushes, Mama'. I want to feel your
hands move my hands. Sometimes the painting
wants to paint itself. Paint, paint, paint… They
called me primate Mama'. They called me
primitive, Mama'. Black man in a suit. Black
man with the cred. With money. Still no respect.
Don't believe them, Mama', Andy is my friend.
We work together. Add, take away. Add, take
away. Add, take away. Andy is dead, Mama'. The
death monster took him. Sick. I feel the vomit
in my throat but it won't come out. Have to
stop. This is the last time. I promise, promise,
promise, promise. All the Hollywood Negroes.
I promise, promise, promise. No, one more
time. So I can paint for you. One last special
canvas for you. I wish I had your shoes. The
red ones. I would paint them. I would paint
anything for you. Beautiful things to help
you remember beautiful things. Puerto Rico.
Everywhere you walked. My beautiful mother.
You know I had to leave, Mom. I know you
understand. I needed to be free. I miss…

He asked me, "Why did you paint this blue?"
Why? Because I wanted to. Always, trying to
trap me. Make me put my foot in my mouth.
Make me sound stupid. Would they ask Miles
if he counted the notes on a page of music?
Black in a white world, Mama'. I get confused
sometimes, Mama'. I'm an outside man. Or am
I an outside-inside man?
My mind is slow and fuzzy, Mama'. Asleep,
awake, I don't know, Mama'. Help me
remember the first one, the first painting we
saw together. If I die now, I want to die with a
painting in my head. If I die, I want to live with
a painting in my head. Like that first painting
we saw together. Come through me and be
mine.
Je marche a l'ombre la mort. Je mange la
nourriture de la mort. Je bois la boisson de la
mort. La mort est avide. Elle demande mon
âme. Elle demande ma liberté. Mon âme
appartient à mon art. Ainsi tu dois mourir, dit la
mort. D'accord la Mort.
Once upon a time, there was a little prince.
He lived in a castle with his mother, his father
and sisters and brothers. This prince had a
magic crown. The crown was only visible
when someone showed him love. Then it was
radiant like a bright star. When someone was
unkind the radiant crown couldn't be seen. This
made the prince very sad. Then one day, a little
yellow bird visited the castle and sat on the
little prince's bed. The yellow bird told him to
never be sad. From that day forward, the crown
would always be visible to him. Dondequiera

que viajaba, allá donde dormía, podía ver su propia corona. El pájaro le dio un beso de buenas noches. El príncipe era feliz.

∞

GISELE: SAMO! I found my SAMO. Permission to be me. Permission to be free. Emancipation. Look. (She turns the finished canvas around to face the headstone.)

(Enter Caretaker)

∞

JM

(Taking the canvas) This is a unique form of graffiti. A beautiful marriage of words and images. I can see strong influence from Jean Michel Basquiat, but I also see a new and fresh approach to using paint and words to examine women's issues within a contemporary landscape. Your color choices are bold without being stereotypic. The pastels feel feminine in the context of the entire composition. Here, I see the rich dialectal language of southern African American voices... yes...perhaps...a homage to Zora Neal Hurston... *Their Eyes Were Watching God.* And beautiful historic reference here. Is this a silhouette of Harriet Tubman? Your painting emotionally moves me. Brava.

∞

GISELE: Hello Jean Michel.

∞

JM

Hello Gisele.

∞

(Gisele and the caretaker look at each other's hands and then hold hands.)

∞

JM

(Holding up a piece of paper) I had the wrong telephone number.

∞

GISELE: Friends?

∞

JM

Friends.

∞

(Exit to opposite areas of the stage)

(Musical interlude: Ravel's Boléro)

CARETAKER & GISELE:

In the end, there was the word
And the word was SAMO
Not SAMBO
Not SAM——O
SAME   OH
Same Old Shit

(Lights Out)

End of Play

Notes

1   *French to English Translation*
    I walk in the shadow of death. I eat death's food. I drink death's
    drink. Death is greedy. It demands my soul. It demands my
    freedom. My soul belongs to my art. Then you must die now death
    says. Okay Death.

2   *Spanish to English Translation*
    Everywhere he traveled, everywhere he slept, he could see his own
    crown. The bird kissed him good night. The prince was happy.

3   Boléro, *composed by Maurice Ravel (1928).*

4. *"Salt Peanuts," Dizzy Gillespie circa 1942.*

Epilogue

Phone Call to John Prine in Heaven
(RIP 2020)

Hi John,

I kept my promise. No. Not that promise. Still working on that one. The promise to find more non-human contents in humans. I looked over your original list: frozen pizzas, ice cubes with hair, and a broken popsicle. I'll spare you the details and tell you the most interesting fact for now. I found eyeballs. Really. Large ones. Hard as rocks. The amazing part is that there were little screen doors in front of the eyeballs and the screen doors were locked. I was so excited. I thought, if I can only unlock the screen doors, these people could see. Not at all. Lots of folks came to unlock the doors: artists, educators, clergy, sanitation workers... An outpouring of support. The doors were unlocked and nothing changed. In fact, the eyeballs had perfect vision. I should have realized that the eyeballs are connected to the moral heart. If there's poison in the heart, the eyeballs will never function with any semblance of humanity. I had to name this inhuman disease 20/20 Blind.

Please tell my Dad, I'll call him later. I'm looking through the photo album with his band buddies. There's someone I don't recognize. I need to ask him about the person playing drums. Percussion is universal. I'm believing this person may not be a person at all. A spirit bringing us back to our human-kind. More later.

Peace & Love, Cesi

"Some Humans Ain't Human," John Prine (2005)

Missing Andi

Inhumanistic

Characters

Ding Dong: Smart house doorbell

Amy Take-Away (Amy): Female carnivorous anthropoid

Detective Diminutive (DD): Male vegan anthropoid

Setting

Amy's underground home

Lights Rise

DING DONG: Ding Dong

AMY: Hi. I'm Amy Take-Away. Call me Amy. Come on in. Watch your step. I just had lunch. There are bones everywhere.

DETECTIVE DIMINUTIVE: I'm

AMY: I know who you are, Detective Diminutive. You're from the small crimes unit.

DETECTIVE DIMINUTIVE: Yes, and…

AMY: And I want to know why my case wasn't sent to Major Crimes.

DETECTIVE DIMINUTIVE: Your spouse

AMY: I prefer you say husband, thank you.

DETECTIVE DIMINUTIVE: Your husband has been missing less than twenty-four hours. It hasn't been established that a crime has been committed.

AMY: (Picking up a bone from the floor and chewing it) A little meat still left on this bone. Hard to chew off meat sfrom femur bones, but I'm still hungry. (Offering the bones to Detective Diminutive) You don't mind if I call you DD, do you?

DETECTIVE DIMINUTIVE: It's Detective Diminutive. I'm a vegan, and I don't eat on the job. Thanks.

AMY: So DD, ever lose a spouse?

DD: Actually

AMY: Every minute… What was his name Ding Dong?

DING DONG: No speak English.

AMY: Don't mind him. He's undocumented, made in China. (Looking at Ding Dong) He's not here to return you to your motherland. He's here about…what's his face.

DD: You don't know the name of your spouse?

AMY: Of course I do. It'll come to me in a moment. Sit down.

DD: I need to take a history and full complaint.

AMY: Ant…Ant…

DING DONG: Andi. That's it. Andi Ant. We had a very brief mixed marriage. I loved him sorta. He was a mutant. I couldn't resist him. And he couldn't resist me. He was attracted to my legs. I have six. He has two. A real turn on.

DD: Kid?

AMY: Of course.

DD: I saw your nest around back. Any offspring still living at home?

AMY: No. Empty nest for now. (Looking at Ding Dong) It's getting cold in here. Turn up the heat please.

DING DONG: (Singing and dancing) *"Turn up the heat. Turn up the heat. Hot hot hot hot."*

DD: What is he doing?

AMY: He's turning up the heat. That's how we do it here.

DD: How many kids do you have?

AMY: Altogether?

DD: (Taking notes) Yes.

AMY: About fifteen thousand over the course of my fertile periods, and I'm still fertile.

DD: Where are the kids?

AMY: Who knows? Each one gets kicked out after birth. Survive or die. That's the kind of mothering I believe in. Move on out. Make room for the next batch.

DD: Describe Andi please.

AMY: He had a teeny tiny human head and a human (Pointing towards her crotch) thing.

DD: Sounds impossible.

AMY: I know. As I said, he's a mutant.

DD: But how…

AMY: Not too many H-mens survived after the last trumpesian nuclear blast. Some survived from gene comingling with anthropoids. We've always been the superior species.

DD: You can turn off the heat now.

(DD stops the singing and dancing)

AMY: I'm preparing for my next fertility period. I need my surroundings to be nice and toasty.

DD: Describe Andi more. Personality? Habits? Anything that might help me determine if he left on his own or he was the victim of foul play.

AMY: As you can see, he was a great provider. I have thighbones, leg bones, and rib bones, even jawbones. (Holding up a human jaw bone) This is the sign of a good husband. Considerate enough to bring jaw bones home for his sweetheart. (Pointing towards the rear of the home) He built a fortified storage hole with more bones on the edge of the property. I have enough human bones to last for the next few hundred years. And he showed me where the human burial grounds are located. Just in case... Not actually burial grounds. He called them, Designated Dead Neighborhoods. When there is scarcity, there is a priority list of chosen survivors based on height in metric numbers and skin complexion-how pale. Isn't that funny? (Speaking to Ding Dong) Time to secure the habitat.

(Ding Dong locks the exits)

DD: What are you doing?

AMY: Just a precaution we take when it's near sundown. (Scratching her legs) I feel environmental light changes in my legs. Ding Dong is here, but basically I'm a female living alone.

DD: A few more questions, and I'll be on my way. (Looking around home) Did you and Andi have a fight, argument, or disagreement before he went missing?

AMY: No, not that I recall.

DING DONG: No.

DD: (Putting away notebook) May I have a glass of purified drinking water please?

AMY: Sure. I'll be back in a jiffy. (Exits)

DD: Ding Dong, you don't need to be afraid to tell...

DING DONG: Get out

AMY: (Offering glass) Here you go. One nice tall recycled glass filled with nuclear waste-free sanitized water, which is better than purified, water. (Looking at Ding Dong) You haven't been telling stories about me have you? (Looking at DD) In five more minutes you'll be off the job, DD.

DD: I'll still be working.

AMY: Not on this case. It will be twenty-four hours. The case of missing Andi can be transferred to the Major Crimes Unit.

DD: I'll finish my report first.

AMY: Sure thing. (Wraps her legs around DD and crushes him) I'll help.

(Ding Dong takes off his head, revealing a human head)

I heard the pods in Major Crimes are juicilicous. Yum Yum, Amy, eat em up. (Speaking to Ding Dong) Amy Take Away says, "Take him away!"

(Ding Dong drags the dead, crushed body out of the house)

(Calling aloud) Crush into small bite-sized pieces Ding Dong. Better for the new babies to chew. (Singing) Andi Andi, A New Day. Andi Andi, A New Day.

(Lights Out)

End of Play

Acknowledgments

The dramatic content in this book was supported and performed by talented artists. Actors, who were members of the organization, performed through the courtesy of Actors' Equity Association: Elizabeth Acosta, E.J. An, Tonia Anderson, Gregory Bastien, Alex Blade Silver, Lucia Bellini, Sara Berg, Paul Bolger, Charles Brice, Jordan Brown, Jill Chenault, China L. Colston, Cara Dekelbaum, Clea DeCrane, Charles Duke, Jose Febus, Michael Flood, Bruce Fuller, Jeannine Foster McKelvia, Charles Everett, Xavier Galva, Mary Hodges, Mike Hodges (Rest in Peace), Kene Holliday, Sarah Keifer, Dianne Kirksey (Rest in Peace) Sharron Lynn, Justin Lord, Clinton Lowe, Rachel Lu, T. Renee Mathis, Kellie Mc Kants, Isreal McKinney Scott, Vernice P. Miller, Sandra Mills Scott, Sam Morales, Marie Elena O'Brien, Sheila Joon Ostadazim, Alex Purcell, Doris Koya Prester, Sadrina Renee, Joshua Redfield, Clea Rivera, David Roberts, Antonia–Sophia Scholz, Joyce Silvester, Johndca Spencer, Kevin Stanfa, Illana Stein, LeVera Sutton, Rosita Timm, Douglas Wade, William Oliver Watkins, and Jared Wilder.

Theatre exists because community exists. We need storytelling and the social interaction it generates for maintaining our humanity. Junelle Carter Bowman, manager of the George Bruce Library, welcomed my work and supported my contributions to the theatre landscape in Harlem, New York City. Many thanks to the community partners who have supported my playmaking in print and in production: Patricia and Roger Barnett, Black Science Fiction Society, Bornquist

Films, Ernestine Dow, Mary Fleischer, Fleetwood Pharmacy, Linda Galietti, Glen Etienne De Lux Hair Gallery, Grandma's Place, Ideacoil, Jacob Restaurant, Florence Kildare, Luis Furniture Style, Loreen Mathis (Rest in Peace), Jim Nuzzo, Sgt. Richard Pierre of the New York City Police Department 26th Precinct, Revolution Books, Ristorante Settepani, Sierra Wellness, Signature Center Bookstore, Sisters Uptown Bookstore, Soho Letterpress, Gloria and Michael Strauss, and Kim Wilson Owens. I remain thankful to the workshop leaders of the Harlem Dramatic Writers Edward Pomerantz, Daniel Judah Sklar, and Zachary Sklar for their continued interest and support of my work.

"Style by Design" was a winner in the Gun Play Competition (2013-2014) founded by Nicole Anderson-Cobb of Samaritan Road Productions. "Entonces Vivamos" premiered at Theatre 54 in New York City as part of Artistic New Directions' Eclectic Evening of Shorts (2015). "Baby Doll," and the complexity of issues related to Domestic Violence, was expanded to podcast and television media through the efforts of Toni Williams, Producer of Art Movz and Brooklyn Savvy (2019).

Some women are part of my life's foundation: my mother Florence, my sister Cheryl, my soul sister Celeste, and my cousin Mickey. Some women support me with friendship, mentoring, and artistic inspiration. Among them Susan Andrasko, Maitefa Angaza, AnnaMaria Assevero, Vicki Ettenger, Blessly Mathews, Sandy Mayzel, Brenda Mills-Hinds, Tania Morales-Velazquez, Maureen Nagle, Ranjini Philip, Vita Rodriguez, Nisi Shawl, Gia Strazzera, LeVera Sutton, and Tobie Stein. Their energy and sincere commitment to advocacy for the arts and equality in all aspects of society gives me hope. I'm grateful to Rachel De Paul, and Felicia Gaon for helping me recognize my suffering from Imposter syndrome. Felicia passed down a hand sewn coat to me. A woman's hand stiches carry traditions and dreams. There are ways to attempt to cross boundaries without words. Brooke Shmuel, Roxie Greenstein…

I'm fortunate to have six brothers who are a steadfast reminder of courageous non-toxic masculinity: Stan, Steve, Charles, Jon Patrick, Michael, and Paul. My children, Hannibal and Rahakmah Bryan help keep my soul alive. My partner, Edward Feeney dances with me in the kitchen and gives me lovely pens with paper. He helps me smile and laugh through life's challenges.

Aqueduct Press has provided a platform for my voice with this second anthology of my work in their Conversation Pieces series. Thank you Timmi, Kath, and Tom. Giving voice, listening, and then reaching for understanding helps humanity move forward.

Cesi Davidson

July 2021

About the Author

Cesi (Cecelia) Davidson holds a doctorate degree in Speech Language Hearing Sciences from the Graduate School and University Center of the City University of New York. After providing therapeutic services for children with communication and learning challenges for over thirty years she reimagined her life as a writer and producing artist. Aqueduct Press published the first anthology of plays with compelling stories for the stage giving voice to her witness of human suffering and triumphs, *Articulation* in 2019. She's founder and curator of Short Plays to Nourish the Mind & Soul, free public theatre in New York City. Cesi is a mother, sister, aunt, partner, friend, and colleague. Without reservation, she believes in human rights and equality. She believes in the power of art to transform and improve our personal and global existence. Her wish is that her words will live beyond her life and stimulate understanding and thoughtful conversation of our one human family.

www.cesiwrites.com/

www.instagram.com/cesiwrites/